THE LAYMAN'S BIBLE COMMENTARY

THE LAYMAN'S BIBLE COMMENTARY
IN TWENTY-FIVE VOLUMES

THE LAYMAN'S
BIBLE COMMENTARY

Balmer H. Kelly, *Editor*

Donald G. Miller   *Associate Editors*   Arnold B. Rhodes

Dwight M. Chalmers, *Editor*, John Knox Press

VOLUME 12

THE BOOK OF
JEREMIAH

THE LAMENTATIONS
OF JEREMIAH

Howard Tillman Kuist

JOHN KNOX PRESS
ATLANTA, GEORGIA

© Marshall C. Dendy 1960

Published in Great Britain by SCM Press Ltd., London.

Fifth printing 1975

Complete set: ISBN: 0-8042-3026-9
This volume: 0-8042-3012-9
Library of Congress Card Number: 59-10454
Printed in the United States of America

PREFACE

The LAYMAN'S BIBLE COMMENTARY is based on the conviction that the Bible has the Word of good news for the whole world. The Bible is not the property of a special group. It is not even the property and concern of the Church alone. It is given to the Church for its own life but also to bring God's offer of life to all mankind—wherever there are ears to hear and hearts to respond.

It is this point of view which binds the separate parts of the LAYMAN'S BIBLE COMMENTARY into a unity. There are many volumes and many writers, coming from varied backgrounds, as is the case with the Bible itself. But also as with the Bible there is a unity of purpose and of faith. The purpose is to clarify the situations and language of the Bible that it may be more and more fully understood. The faith is that in the Bible there is essentially one Word, one message of salvation, one gospel.

The LAYMAN'S BIBLE COMMENTARY is designed to be a concise non-technical guide for the layman in personal study of his own Bible. Therefore, no biblical text is printed along with the comment upon it. This commentary will have done its work precisely to the degree in which it moves its readers to take up the Bible for themselves.

The writers have used the Revised Standard Version of the Bible as their basic text. Occasionally they have differed from this translation. Where this is the case they have given their reasons. In the main, no attempt has been made either to justify the wording of the Revised Standard Version or to compare it with other translations.

One objective in this commentary is to provide the most helpful explanation of fundamental matters in simple up-to-date terms. Exhaustive treatment of subjects has not been undertaken.

In our age knowledge of the Bible is perilously low. At the same time there are signs that many people are longing for help in getting such knowledge. Knowledge of and about the Bible is, of course, not enough. The grace of God and the work of the Holy Spirit are essential to the renewal of life through the Scriptures. It is in the happy confidence that the great hunger for the Word is a sign of God's grace already operating within men, and that the Spirit works most wonderfully where the Word is familiarly known, that this commentary has been written and published.

THE EDITORS AND
THE PUBLISHERS

THE BOOK OF
JEREMIAH

INTRODUCTION

The Prophet Jeremiah

Michelangelo, in his well-known portrayal in the Sistine Chapel, pictures the prophet Jeremiah as "a man of sorrows, and acquainted with grief" yet a man of massive strength, whose broad right shoulder is bowed beneath a weighty burden. Just behind and above that shoulder stands a tragic daughter of Zion, a figure of abject despair, who portrays the prophet's burden: God's alienated, rebellious Covenant people. But behind the prophet's elevated left shoulder is the profile of a chastened son of Judah who gazes toward but beyond this smitten woman to a point on the distant horizon, the divine glow of which is reflected upon his countenance. In one single portrait the great master has given classic expression to the two most typical characteristics of Jeremiah. The one identifies the man from Anathoth as a prophet of inevitable doom to a stiff-necked generation. The other distinguishes him as a true herald of the everlasting gospel. Jeremiah is indeed a figure of tragic sorrow, yet also a man of unconquerable hope.

The Career of Jeremiah

Little is known about the beginning or the end of Jeremiah's life. He was born about 650 B.C. at Anathoth, a priestly city in the land of Benjamin, some three miles northeast of Jerusalem. His father's name was Hilkiah, a priest of the line of Abiathar who had been exiled to Anathoth by Solomon (I Kings 1 and 2). About 626 B.C. Jeremiah was called of God to be a prophet (Jeremiah 1). How far he identified himself with the reforms of Josiah described in II Kings 22 and 23 is uncertain. At any rate, he saw that these attempts at outward reform were insufficient (see, for example, Jer. 3:6-10). He preached instead a religion of the heart and proclaimed that the regeneration of the nation must be wrought out at the deeper level of ethical righteousness.

According to II Chronicles 35:24-25, Jeremiah considered the death of Josiah to be a tragic event of the first order.

Conflict is the keynote of Jeremiah's public career. The narrative parts of the book are almost completely devoted to his conflicts. His life was threatened by his own people at Anathoth for pressing home the claims of the Covenant God, an insistence which apparently clashed with local home interest (Jer. 11:21-23). He was tried for his life by the priests and prophets for preaching a daring sermon in the Temple. Even after his vindication he had to be protected by Ahikam, a prince of Judah (Jer. 26:24). He was put in the stocks overnight by Pashhur, a priest, for openly predicting by a symbolic act the destruction of Jerusalem (Jer. 20:1-6). He and Baruch his scribe had to flee to save their lives from King Jehoiakim after Baruch had read in public the contents of a scroll on which Jeremiah's prophecies for the preceding twenty-three years had been written (Jer. 36). He was publicly humiliated by Hananiah, a prophet from Gibeon, for advocating a policy of submission to Babylon (Jer. 27-28). Jeremiah was hounded by the princes of the house of Judah, who lowered him into a cistern in the mire of which he certainly would have perished had he not been saved, at the last minute, by Ebed-melech, the Ethiopian servant of King Zedekiah (Jer. 38). At the time of the fall of Jerusalem, Jeremiah could have gone to Babylon as the guest of the king, but he preferred instead to cast his lot with the poorest people, those who were left in Judah to care for the land. A tradition about Jeremiah preserved in the apocryphal book called "The Lives of the Prophets" declares that he was stoned to death by the people of the remnant at Tahpanhes in Egypt. And so, from first to last, Jeremiah devoted himself utterly to his people in the name of the Lord only to be rejected by them, a fact which was foreshadowed in the words which attended his call to a prophetic career (Jer. 1:18-19).

The Times of Jeremiah

Jeremiah presents such a tragic figure because he understood, perhaps better than any other single individual, the meaning of what was a period of culminating tragedy for the Covenant people.

Jeremiah's public ministry, of four decades (626-587 B.C.), occurred during a time of decisive struggle among the civilizations of the Near East. Jeremiah's people were drawn into the vortex of this struggle because their land occupied a central position in the whole region known as "the Fertile Crescent." Any good map of this region shows how Palestine, like a bridge, is a commercial and military link between the north and the south and between the Mediterranean Sea to the west and the Arabian Desert to the east. This bridge-land was populated in Jeremiah's day by peoples of diverse cultural traditions and intense national loyalties.

A map of the region as it was in the seventh century presents a picture like this: Syria at the northeast, its capital at Damascus (49:23-27); Tyre and Sidon, Phoenician city-states, at the northwest on the Mediterranean (27:1-3); the Moabites and Ammonites, pastoral peoples at the fringes of the desert to the east of the Jordan (48:1—49:6); the Edomites, secure in their rugged cliffs which border on the Arabah to the south (49:7-22); the Philistines, the trading peoples on the seacoast to the southwest (ch. 47); Judah, its capital at Jerusalem, an agricultural state at the center. Israel (Samaria) was already in captivity (721 B.C.; see Jer. 2:14-15).

How were these smaller nationalities to hold out against the great empires, Egypt to the south (ch. 46) and Assyria and Babylonia to the north and east (chs. 50-51), at a time of decisive shift in the center of military and political gravity to Babylon? This crucial question dictated national and international policy during the tumultuous decades of Jeremiah's ministry. That he addressed the claims of God to "all the nations" is written as though in large print in the book. Particularly is this emphasized in chapter 25 and in chapters 46-51 (see comments on these chapters).

During this period one crisis followed another in the lands of the Fertile Crescent. Early in Jeremiah's ministry the security of Judah was threatened by an unnamed foe from the north (chs. 4, 5, 6), identified by some historians as Scythian hordes who penetrated along the seacoast as far as Gaza. During the turmoil which followed the fall of Nineveh in 612 B.C., the Assyrian Empire was destroyed, never to rise again. Egypt then made a new bid for empire in the east. Pharaoh Neco's mercenary legions marched northward. King Josiah of Judah, attempting to cut him off at Megiddo, perished in 609 B.C. The Egyptian king soon dethroned Jehoahaz, third son of Josiah in age, whom the people had proclaimed king of Judah, and sent him in chains a prisoner to Egypt. In his stead Pharaoh Neco elevated Eliakim, the elder brother of Jehoahaz, to the throne of Judah and changed his name to Jehoiakim. The Egyptian army then pushed northward. At Carchemish on the Euphrates, Nebuchadnezzar of Babylon decisively defeated the Egyptians in 605 B.C. This was the fourth year of King Jehoiakim of Judah (chs. 25, 36, 45, 46), who now became a vassal of Babylon. Upon his death in 598 B.C., he was succeeded by his son Jehoiachin, who reigned only three months. Conditions in Judah had deteriorated so rapidly that Nebuchadnezzar led his troops to Jerusalem and in the same year deported Jehoiachin and the queen mother to Babylon, with ten thousand of the best people of the land.

The Babylonian king then appointed Mattaniah, one of Josiah's younger sons, as king and changed his name to Zedekiah. But Zedekiah failed to fulfill his oath of allegiance. In 589 B.C., Nebuchadnezzar sent his armies against Judah. They besieged the Holy City for eighteen months before a breach was made in the walls (chs. 21, 34, 37, 38; 39:1-2). The city and the Temple of Solomon were destroyed, the king and his princes were captured, and all but the poorest people of the land were deported (chs. 39, 52). A governor, named Gedaliah, was appointed to keep order. Shortly after he had set up his government at Mizpah, Gedaliah was slain. The miserable remnant of the people, fearing revenge, fled to Egypt, taking with them Jeremiah the prophet and Baruch his faithful scribe (chs. 40-44).

The following chronological table indicates the sequence of these events and gives the parallel passages in the historical books:

CHRONOLOGICAL TABLE

Reign of Josiah, 31 years	640-609 B.C.
II Kings 22:1—23:30	
II Chronicles 34, 35	
Reforms of Josiah advanced	622 B.C.
Fall of Nineveh	612 B.C.
Battle of Megiddo, Death of Josiah	609 B.C.
Reign of Jehoahaz, 3 months	609 B.C.
II Kings 23:31-35	
II Chronicles 36:1-4	

Reign of Jehoiakim, 11 years II Kings 23:36—24:7 II Chronicles 36:4-8	609-598 B.C.
Battle of Carchemish	605 B.C.
Reign of Jehoiachin, 3 months II Kings 24:8-17 II Chronicles 36:9-10	598-597 B.C.
The ten thousand deported to Babylon	598-597 B.C.
Reign of Zedekiah, 11 years II Kings 24:18—25:30 Jeremiah 52:1-34 II Chronicles 36:11-21	597-587 B.C.
The siege of Jerusalem begun	589 B.C.
The Temple burned and city destroyed	587 B.C.
Second deportation to Babylon	587 B.C.

Jeremiah's period is indeed an era of culminating tragedy. What the prophet of Anathoth had sought to avert came to pass. To Jeremiah the fall of Jerusalem was far more than a military or political catastrophe. To him it was a terrible moral and spiritual calamity which overtook his headstrong and rebellious generation. Yet even in disaster the prophet was not without hope. Having proclaimed the word of God to the Covenant people for four decades, having suffered with them during the siege, and having watched with them the lingering agony of their dissolution as a nation, he was granted finally to see the faithfulness of the God of his fathers at work in a new way. His darkest hour became the moment of his brightest hope in his vision of the new Covenant (31:31-34).

Jeremiah knew that the foundations had been shaken in judgment, but he saw nevertheless that unfathomed depths of divine mercy still remained. The Covenant people, in very deed, had spurned and had rejected the Covenant-keeping God. They were now suffering exile from their homeland. But, true to himself, God would be faithful to his people. He was now offering to make their future destiny even more glorious than he had promised. He was coming to them with better promises by establishing for them a new Covenant. In the end, the prophet of Judah's doom had become the herald of the everlasting gospel.

Stages in the Making of the Book of Jeremiah

The times of Jeremiah were out of joint and so were the times which followed. This may account, in some measure at least, for the disjointed contents of the book which interprets those times. The casual reader today soon recognizes that the parts are not arranged in any precise chronological order. The trained interpreter is confounded by many strange incongruities in the condition of the text. Martin Luther declared of the prophecy, "We must not trouble ourselves about the order, or allow the want of order to hinder us." Yet we should seek to learn as much as possible of how this book, as we know it, came to be.

Beginning with Jeremiah himself, it is possible to trace several stages in the making of the book, each of which made a contribution to its present structural arrangement.

From the time that Jeremiah dictated his earlier messages to Baruch on the first scroll (see ch. 36) until the canonical book called Jeremiah had taken permanent shape, various builders had a hand in its construction. The making of the book apparently began in the fourth year of Jehoiakim when, to quote Baruch, Jeremiah "dictated all these words to me, while I wrote them with ink on the scroll" (36:18). After Jehoiakim burned this scroll in the fire, we are told that he sought to "seize Baruch the secretary and Jeremiah the prophet, but the LORD hid them" (36:26). Then Jeremiah took another scroll and gave it to Baruch. In addition to the words on the first scroll, "many similar words were added" to this second scroll (36:32). All we know about the contents of either of these scrolls is suggested by the words in 36:2: "Take a scroll and write on it all the words that I have spoken to you against Israel and Judah and all the nations, from the day I spoke to you, from the days of Josiah until today" (a period of about 23 years). This indicates that the second scroll contained an expanded account of Jeremiah's messages and experiences during the first half of his prophetic career. In view of these facts it would not be too much to say that the contents of this second scroll (all undated except at 3:6) must have provided most of the materials which came to be built into the finished edifice known as Jeremiah chapters 1-20.

A second discernible stage in the making of the book can also be recognized by an observing reader. Someone besides Jeremiah, presumably Baruch, Jeremiah's faithful scribe, took a hand in setting down his own record of what Jeremiah had said and done. One evidence of this is the contrast between chapters 1-20 and chapters 21-52 in the expressions which refer to the prophet. Any observant reader will soon recognize that the characteristic references to Jeremiah in the earlier part of the book are in the first person; for instance, "The word of the LORD came to *me*," as though in these passages Jeremiah himself is speaking. In such cases may we not be dealing with the actual words of Jeremiah as he pronounced them to his scribe? (Yet see 11:1, 6; 14:1, 11; 18:1, 5.) But beginning at chapter 21 the characteristic formula is in the third person, "The word of the LORD came to *Jeremiah*," and the specific mode of referring to the speaker or actor is "to Jeremiah the prophet," instead of "to me" as in chapters 1-20. (Yet see 24:4; 27:2; 28:1.) The prominence of Baruch in chapter 45 and elsewhere suggests that he had kept his own "memoirs" even after the fall of Jerusalem, and it would have been natural for him to refer to Jeremiah in the third person in these "memoirs." How much we owe to this devoted scribe for recording and preserving a faithful record of Jeremiah's words and deeds, as well as for their arrangement, will perhaps never be known. We do know, however, that as a reward for all the risks he took as Jeremiah's fellow worker he received the divine promise: "but I will give you your life as a prize of war in all places to which you may go" (45:5). The work of Baruch the scribe is recognizable in that part of the edifice known as Jeremiah 21-52. He not only contributed materials but may have arranged certain parts in a permanent sequence. The clearest examples of such handiwork may be recognized within the scope of such passages as chapters 26-29; 37-38; and 42-44. The parts composed in the first person are usually referred to as autobiographic and those written in the third person as biographic.

Still a third stage in the making of this rugged book may be recognized. Considering the chaotic times of Jeremiah's public ministry, culminating in the siege and fall of Jerusalem, the deportation of the people to Babylon, and the flight of the remnant to Egypt, it is a marvel that any records written within this period survived at all. Who, then, took up the making of this book where Jeremiah and Baruch left off? That other hands besides those of Jeremiah and Baruch had an active part in

shaping the materials of the book into its permanent and final
arrangement is indicated by evidence of various kinds. Here the
reader who desires to explore the more intricate aspects of this
scholar's puzzle needs the more specialized guidance which he
will find in the historical works listed at the end of the first
volume of the LAYMAN'S BIBLE COMMENTARY. There he will be
introduced to such types of evidence as the following: (1) The
striking parallels between the language of the Books of Jeremiah
and Deuteronomy. (2) The editorial headings of certain chapters, such as 34, 35, 40, 44. (3) The grouping of certain parts
which must once have existed separately as smaller collections
before they were incorporated into the permanent structure of
the book, like chapters 21-23; 30-33; 46-49; 50-51. (4) Passages like 10:1-11 and 10:12-16 (parallel to 51:15-19), which
stem apparently from a time well within the period of the
Exile. (5) The significant differences between the Hebrew and
Greek texts of Jeremiah both in subject matter and order of
parts. The Greek text (otherwise known as the Septuagint, a translation made within the two centuries before Christ) is about one-
eighth shorter than the Hebrew text. Its arrangement of parts, too,
is strikingly different from the Hebrew text, particularly in the
messages addressed to foreign nations. These messages are found
in the Hebrew text (and so in our English Bible) in chapters
46-51. In the Greek text they are introduced at 25:13, immediately before Jeremiah's symbolic Wine Cup Utterance addressed to the nations (see comments on this section). No final
answer to these differences between the Hebrew and Greek texts
has as yet been offered. Yet these two texts themselves provide,
in small part at least, some answer. Two editions of the Hebrew
text of Jeremiah seem to have been available when the Greek
translation was made, and, of the two, that used by the Greek
translators was the shorter.

To sum up: Taken together these five types of evidence indicate that the third stage in the making of the Book of Jeremiah,
like the first two stages, was a gradual process. Other faithful
builders entered into the labors of Jeremiah and Baruch. What
Jeremiah himself had "dictated" and Baruch had written "with
ink on the scroll," what Baruch also had recorded on his own
part, was now compiled by their successors with other prophetic
materials which meanwhile had accumulated (for example, see
comments on 10:25; 30:1-3; 33:14-26). These component parts

were fashioned, together with editorial headings, into a larger whole and so assumed the permanent form which came to be known as "Jeremiah." It was in this form that the book was incorporated with Isaiah, Ezekiel, and the Book of the Twelve into "The Latter Prophets," and thus into the Hebrew Canon.

And so it came to pass, through the human instrumentality of Jeremiah, Baruch, and other men of God, that the word of the Lord to the Covenant people was recorded, compiled, and preserved. Meanwhile divine influences also had been at work, for the same God who had formed Jeremiah to be a prophet strikingly fulfilled the words of the first vision which attended Jeremiah's call, "for I am watching over my word to perform it" (1:12). What God had said, God had done. And what God did in the times of Jeremiah was faithfully recorded for all men to read in the book called Jeremiah. This book, having been incorporated as one of the Prophets in the Old Testament, has become our goodly heritage in Holy Scripture: the word of the Lord to the people of the new Covenant.

The Structure of the Book

There are evidences of design which indicate that the composition of this book is not so strange after all. Aside from the preface (1:1-3) and the appendix (52:1-34), seven major areas form the total layout of the parts. These are:

Earlier Discourses (Autobiographic)	Chapters 1-10
Narratives and Pronouncements (Autobiographic)	
	Chapters 11-20
Narratives and Pronouncements (Biographic)	Chapters 21-29
Prophetic Utterances and Narratives (Biographic)	
	Chapters 30-39
Historical Narratives (Biographic)	Chapters 40-44
Dated Dialogue (Biographic)	Chapter 45
Prophetic Discourses (Biographic)	Chapters 46-51

For more detailed treatment, the Outline should be consulted. The following section deals with the main features of each of the main areas of the book.

Chapters 1-10: Earlier Discourses (Autobiographic)
Main Topic: Jeremiah Proclaims Judah's Guilt

The first ten chapters of the book are all in discourse form.
Following the preface (1:1-3), chapter 1 relates the call and
commission of Jeremiah. Chapters 2 and 3 consist of occasional
utterances (note the single reference to time in 3:6). The
prophet's pointed questions which probe the guilt of his people
(ch. 2) and the recurring calls to "return" (ch. 3) suggest the
topical affinities of these utterances designed to stir the people
to repentance. In chapters 4, 5, 6 two aspects of Judah's plight
are treated in an alternating sequence. One of these main topics
is Judah's peril from an unnamed enemy "from the north." The
alternating topic, which emphasizes the peril threatening the
Covenant people from within, is Judah's "stubborn and rebellious heart" (5:23). Chapters 7-10 present another topical
grouping of parts. In 7:1-15 the main points of Jeremiah's daring Temple Sermon are elaborated. The succeeding utterances
in chapters 7-10 strongly reiterate the major notes of the
Temple Sermon, even though these utterances must have been
delivered at many different moments in the prophet's earlier ministry. One significant passage (10:1-16) could hardly have been
spoken by Jeremiah at all since it stems from a time deep in
the Exile (see comment on 10:1-16). It appears to have been
placed here by the final compilers, as it emphasizes a similar
topic: The Covenant people, now in exile, are encouraged to
worship the one true God.

The reader of the Revised Standard Version will have observed that the text of Jeremiah 1-10 is presented in some cases
as prose and in others as poetry. These two forms of writing,
prose and poetry, are characteristic of the Hebrew text throughout the whole book. The poetic parts indicate that Jeremiah
frequently gave a lyrical, ecstatic tone to his utterances by speaking in elegiac meter (meter in which a line of three accents or
beats is followed by a line of two beats). A typical example of
such rhythm may be observed in the utterance at the opening
of chapter 2:

> I remember   the devotion   of your youth,
>   your love   as a bride,
> how you followed   me   in the wilderness,
>   in a land   not sown.

Chapters 11-20: Narratives and Pronouncements
(Autobiographic)
Main Topics: Jeremiah's Confessions and Judah's Approaching Doom

Chapters 11-20, all undated, record typical personal experiences of Jeremiah. Intermixed with these narratives, chiefly autobiographic, are stern pronouncements of doom upon the Covenant people, along with occasional editorial headings. Two dominant features characterize this part of the book. The one is usually referred to as "The Confessions of Jeremiah," beginning with his heartbreak over the treachery of his own people at Anathoth (11:18-23 and 12:1-6) and concluding with his overnight experience in the stocks (20:1-18). Other confessional passages are 15:10-21; 17:14-18; 18:18-23; 20:7-18. Still other autobiographic passages are 11:6-17; 13:1-27; 16:1-9; 18:1-12; 19:1-15.

The other primary topical feature of this area is the emphasis on Judah's approaching doom. The passages in which this note is stressed are 12:7-17; 14:1—15:9; 16:10-21; 17:1-13; 18:13-17. Occasional editorial headings, doubtless the work of the final compilers, also punctuate this part of the book, as for example at 11:1; 14:1; 18:1.

No single area within the range of prophetic literature lays bare the inner life of a man of God more frankly or lucidly than this section of the book. Jeremiah's confessions disclose both the depth and the height of emotion, his fightings without and fears within, his mental stress and spiritual anguish in which his tender communings with God are sometimes punctuated by bitter questionings and even by a curse. At the same time the reader is made aware of the urgent concern of the prophet for his people, as he exposes their shallow regard for God's claims and their ingrained apostasy which made inevitable their doom.

Chapters 21-29: Narratives and Pronouncements (Biographic)
Main Topic: Jeremiah and the Kings, Prophets, and Priests

A new section of the book begins at 21:1 where, as elsewhere in the structure, topical emphasis prevails over strict historical sequence. The dominant feature within this area of the book is the emphatic attention given to Jeremiah's relations to the civil and religious leaders of his people: the kings of Judah, the prophets, the priests, and the leaders of the people in exile. In the composition of this section, apparently no attempt was made to arrange the narrative into any recognizable chronological sequence, as a review of the successive headings indicates.

The kings of Judah are dealt with first: Zedekiah (21:1-10), and other sons of Josiah, including also Josiah's grandson Jehoiachin (Coniah), all of whom are addressed as members of the "house of the king of Judah" (21:11—23:8). The "prophets" and exiles are then addressed (23:9—24:10). Two different situations in which King Jehoiakim is involved follow (chs. 25 and 26, of which 26 is the earlier). Events and discourses dated during the reign of Zedekiah conclude the section. Final warnings are given, first to the surrounding nations (27:1-11); then to King Zedekiah (27:12-15); to priests and people (27:16-22); to Hananiah, the prophet of Gibeon (28:1-17); and finally, to the exiles (29:1-32).

Here, from a broad perspective, various aspects of Jeremiah's prophetic message are emphasized. In biographic composition he is presented in the role of a statesman who sees clearly the political as well as the moral situation in which his nation is involved. For the first time in the book the name of Nebuchadnezzar (sometimes spelled Nebuchadrezzar), king of Babylon, is introduced (21:2). From here on, the role of Jeremiah as "a prophet to the nations" looms large in the foreground of the action. At the same time Babylon is proclaimed to be the "enemy from the north" and the instrument of the Lord's wrath against the Covenant people (21:3-7; 25:8-9). But an even more significant theological feature overshadows the whole situation as presented in chapters 21-29. The "house of the king of Judah" —that is, the dynasty of David—is shown to be chastised by the "outstretched hand and strong arm" of the Lord (21:5, 10, 13-14; 22:6-9, 20-23); "Wrath has gone forth, a whirling tempest," which is about to burst upon the head of the wicked (23:19); the Lord has "an indictment against the nations; he is entering into judgment with all flesh" (25:31); the Lord of hosts, the God of Israel, by his outstretched arm, has appointed Nebuchadnezzar, the king of Babylon, his "servant" over the nations. All the nations are to "serve" Babylon, and wear this yoke as by divine decree (27:1-7). As for the captives in Babylon, they are to build houses and plant gardens and seek the peace of their captors. Even so, they should know that they are not forsaken, for the Lord's plans for them are "plans for welfare and not for evil," to give them hope in their latter end (29: 1-14). The word of the Lord in the mouth of Jeremiah—the stern note of impending judgment, not unmingled with hope—constitutes the absorbing center of interest in these otherwise disjointed chapters.

Chapters 30-39: Prophetic Utterances and Narratives
(Biographic)
Main Topic: The Siege and Fall of Jerusalem

The most characteristic heading used to introduce the contents of chapters 30-39 is "The word of the LORD came to Jeremiah." Here Jeremiah is usually referred to as "the prophet" (yet see 31:26; 32:6-25; 35:3-5). These headings identify the composition in this area of the book as biographic.

It is quite apparent, too, that a topical interest took priority over any chronological considerations in the composition of this section, for no attempt seems to have been made to relate the main parts in any temporal sequence. The point of view of chapters 30-31 is distinctly that of the period after the fall of Jerusalem. Chapters 32-33 are dated late during the siege. Chapter 34 is timed midway during the siege. Chapters 35 and 36 turn the attention of the reader to the reign of Jehoiakim. The events of chapter 36 are recorded as taking place during the fourth and fifth years of Jehoiakim (36:1, 9). Chapters 37 and 38 record the trying experiences of Jeremiah during the latter part of the siege, while chapter 39 concludes the section by describing the fall of Jerusalem to the Babylonian army.

Taken together chapters 30-33 are usually referred to as "The Book of Consolation," where the most hopeful utterances of Jeremiah are found. Chapter 34, with chapters 37-39, might well be called "The Book of Disaster," for here the reader is shown how the morale of king, princes, and people deteriorated during the prolonged months of the siege, while the courage and rugged faith of the prophet were put to the severest tests. Curiously enough, chapters 35 and 36 transport the reader back to events which occurred about a decade and a half before the siege of Jerusalem, during the reign of Jehoiakim, but the topical emphasis is not entirely broken, for chapter 35 records an event which occurred while Jerusalem and the region nearby were beleaguered by Babylonian troops (35:11; see comment). No rational explanation can be given for the position of chapter 36 in this sequence.

This section performs the significant function of a bridge between the Old and the New Testaments of the Bible. In fundamental agreement with all the prophets, Jeremiah proclaimed that the Covenant people were chosen by the living God to bear witness to his redemptive purpose for the world. Therefore their destiny was not to be concluded with Judah's dissolution as a state. The flames that consumed Jerusalem and its Temple were to be a purifying fire for these Covenant people. From the Exile they would return to their own land as a chastened people. In the more distant future God's people would live and move and have their being within the privileges of a new Covenant.

Chapters 40-44: Historical Narratives (Biographic)
Main Topic: Judah After the Fall of Jerusalem

The preface to the Book of Jeremiah (1:1-3) apparently was meant to serve as a heading to chapters 1-39, for it relates the work of Jeremiah to the three major kings of the period, Josiah, Jehoiakim, and Zedekiah, "until the captivity of Jerusalem." Chapters 40-44, written in the form of biographical narrative, seem to have existed as an independent unit before they were attached to the contents in chapters 1-39. They appear to have been added here so that the book might include an account of Jeremiah's activities after the fall of Jerusalem. Although 40:7—41:18 does not mention Jeremiah, the narrative deals with events connected with Gedaliah's governorship at Mizpah and his tragic death which led to the chaotic situation in which Jeremiah is found in chapters 42-44. After a ten-day period of prayer Jeremiah counseled the remnant to stay in the land of Judah (42:1-22). The remnant rejected his word and took him with them to Egypt (43:1-7). By means of an extraordinary symbolic act he dramatized the futility of this attempt to escape from war and captivity (43:8-13). A final picture of Jeremiah presents his honest but brokenhearted attempt to restrain the women of the remnant from worshiping the queen of heaven (44:1-30).

Chapter 45: Dated Dialogue (Biographic)
Main Topic: Jeremiah Counsels Baruch

This brief exchange between Jeremiah and his scribe gives further biographical light on the relations between the two men.

If read in connection with 36:8, as is suggested by the heading of chapter 45, this dialogue illuminates the period of about a year during which the first scroll was being prepared. Some interpreters prefer to ignore the heading of this chapter and to think of the event described here as the final charge of Jeremiah to Baruch before the two were separated after the fall of Jerusalem. In this way they would account for the position of the chapter in connection with the events described in chapters 40-44.

Chapters 46-51: Prophetic Discourses (Biographic)
Main Topic: The Word of the Lord to the Nations

The intricate problem of accounting for the striking differences between the Hebrew text and the Greek text of the Book of Jeremiah, in connection with the messages addressed to foreign nations, is discussed in the comment on chapter 25.

That Jeremiah was true to his commission as a prophet "to the nations" is to be seen in his active role as a statesman who saw more clearly than anyone else in his day the burning moral and spiritual issues involved in the relations between the Covenant people and the other peoples of the Fertile Crescent. How much of the content of chapters 46-51 stems from Jeremiah himself and how much from other prophetic materials which had accumulated about his messages has been keenly debated because the evidence is inconclusive. Yet such biographic details as are found here, in the imagery (for example, 46:3-6), the questions (for example, 46:7, 15), point of view (for example, 51:59-64), and emphasis (for example, 47:1-7), correspond so strikingly to those of Jeremiah in the earlier autobiographic parts that these messages in their basic appeal ring with the same characteristic fervor and veracity. They certainly belong to the Book of Jeremiah.

Chapter 52: An Historical Appendix (Biographic)
Main Topic: The Fall of Jerusalem

This chapter, parallel in word and thought to II Kings 25, should be read in connection with Jeremiah 39. These three passages taken together provide the reader with the source materials for the fall of Jerusalem in 587 B.C. and other items connected with succeeding events.

The Message of Jeremiah

Jeremiah's ministry to his people was distinctive. Yet it must be remembered that he belonged heart and soul to a great succession of prophets who proclaimed the word of the Lord. As compared to the work of the earliest prophets, Jeremiah's protest against the worship of Baal was not as dramatic as that of Elijah on Mount Carmel (I Kings 18), but it was none the less burning and real (Jer. 2:23-25; 11:9-17). Jeremiah was as unsparing of Jehoiakim's opulent greed (Jer. 22:13-19) as the Tishbite was of Ahab's avarice (I Kings 21:17-24). As compared to the last of the prophets, Jeremiah shows ethical sensitivity fully as sharp as that of John the Baptist, and his call to his people to "bear fruits that befit repentance" (Luke 3:8) was just as urgent. The word of the Lord's wrath in the mouth of each was unsparing as fire (Jer. 5:14; 11:16; Matt. 3:7-12; Luke 3:15-17). Each suffered violence for having unmasked an unworthy figure who was on the throne (Jer. 36:20-31; 38:1-13; Mark 6:14-29; Matt. 14:1-12).

Like Hosea, Jeremiah proclaimed the Covenant relation between God and his people to be that of a marriage bond in which God had proved himself to be a faithful Husband (2:1-2; 3:1-13; 31:32; Hosea, chs. 1-2). Both prophets rebuked the infidelity of the house of Israel by using the symbols of adultery and harlotry. Like Amos, Jeremiah lashed out against the sins of the surrounding nations as well as against those of his own people (chs. 25 and 46-49; Amos, chs. 1-2). Both prophets drew imagery from agricultural life to vivify their messages (for example, Jer. 24:1-10; Amos 8:1-3). Both prophets affirmed that the Lord of Hosts is the sovereign God over all nature and peoples (see, for example, Jer. 32:16-25; Amos 4:13). Each was threatened with violence, being sharply told, "You shall not prophesy" (Jer. 11:21; Amos 2:12; 7:12-13).

Like Micah, Jeremiah pronounced startling and provocative words about the house of the Lord and the city of Jerusalem (Jer. 26:1-15; 7:1-15; Micah 3:9-12). Jeremiah was put on trial for his life because he had "prophesied against this city." But certain elders of the land cited the favorable response of Hezekiah and the people of Judah to the pronouncement of Micah. The influence of this century-old precedent led to the vindication of

Jeremiah as one who had "spoken . . . in the name of the LORD" (Jer. 26:16-19). It also won for him the protection of a powerful prince (26:24).

Jeremiah's people had inherited from Isaiah's day a fanatical belief that they were secure as long as the house of the Lord was in their midst. At the time of the Assyrian siege in 722 B.C., Isaiah had promised his people that "like birds hovering" so the Lord would protect Jerusalem (Isa. 31:5), and that Zion was like an immovable tent whose stakes would never be plucked up (Isa. 33:20). But the people of Isaiah's day, having repented in sackcloth and ashes, actually were delivered (Isa., ch. 37). Now, more than a century later, the people of Jerusalem were looking upon the Temple as a sort of protective charm, potent no matter how they lived or what they did. Jeremiah reminded them that, as God had destroyed Shiloh several centuries earlier, so he would destroy both house and city unless they met the strict ethical conditions of his Covenant with them (Jer. 7:8-15; I Sam. 4:1-22).

Jeremiah and his contemporary Ezekiel (who was taken with the captives to Babylon in 597 B.C.) were equally severe in their denunciations of Judah's infidelity (Jer. 27:16—28:17; 29:15-32; Ezek. 2:1—3:27). Each was certain that Zedekiah's futile resistance in breaking his oath to Nebuchadnezzar would be disastrous (Jer. 21:1-10; Ezek. 17). But each was sure that a real restoration awaited the chastened captives (Jer. 31; Ezek. 37).

This confidence of Jeremiah in future restoration reached far beyond mere return from exile. It was linked with what may well be regarded as the most distinctive note in Jeremiah's message. In the past, collective responsibility for transgressions of the Covenant had been a general assumption. The Covenant people, or the tribe, or the family, as including the individual, was responsible. But now the embittered exiles were challenging this assumption. Ezekiel (18:1-4) and Jeremiah (31:29-30) had an answer for them. From now on, "every one shall die for his own sin; each man who eats sour grapes, his teeth shall be set on edge." Jeremiah's most significant single teaching is introduced here at the precise moment when the ethical significance of the fall of Jerusalem could be most clearly seen. He now gave to his people a vision of God's future dealings with his people, by unfolding to their jaded spirits the meaning of the new Covenant (see comment on 31:31-34).

The influence of Jeremiah's message on those who gave us the New Testament is to be measured by the way in which his words appear in their writings. There are some forty direct quotations or allusions to the language of the book in the New Testament. These can be found quite readily in the cross-reference footnotes in the Revised Standard Version. Twenty of them are in the Revelation. Most of them are apocalyptic descriptions of the fall of Babylon. Stephen's reference to worship of "the host of heaven" by the ancient Israelites (Acts 7:42) is reminiscent of Jeremiah 19:13, and the description of his hearers as a "stiff-necked people, uncircumcised in heart and ears" (Acts 7:51) is characteristic of Jeremiah (9:26 and 6:10). In Romans 9:19-21 Paul makes use of Jeremiah's metaphor of the potter and the clay to express his confidence in the justice and sovereignty of the Almighty (Jer. 18:1-4; see also I Cor. 1:31; II Cor. 10:17; I Thess. 2:4).

But perhaps the most significant relations of all between this prophet and the New Testament are those which connect Jeremiah of Anathoth and Jesus of Nazareth. It is reported in the Gospel according to Matthew (16:13-14) that at Caesarea Philippi, when Jesus asked his disciples, "Who do men say that the Son of man is?", they replied, "Some say . . . Jeremiah." The parallels between these two characters are striking. Both grew up in little country towns, and each was rejected by his own people. Both of them loved the common people and wept over them. Each was opposed severely by the leaders of his day. Each made the Temple at Jerusalem a center for his teaching. When Jesus cleansed Herod's Temple he referred to Jeremiah's words, "Has this house, which is called by my name, become a den of robbers in your eyes?" (Jer. 7:11) as to something actually accomplished (Matt. 21:13).

But there is an end to these parallels between Jeremiah and Jesus. Under pressure Jeremiah winced, or uttered vindictive words against his enemies such as, "Pull them out like sheep for the slaughter" (Jer. 12:3), or "Forgive not their iniquity" (18:23). Jesus, as he suffered the worst at the hands of his enemies, breathed the prayer, "Father, forgive them; for they know not what they do" (Luke 23:34).

OUTLINE

The Fidelity of the Rechabites (35:1-19)
Jeremiah and the Two Scrolls (36:1-32)
Jeremiah and the Siege of Jerusalem (37:1—38:28)
The Fall of Jerusalem (39:1—40:6)

Historical Narratives (Biographic). Jeremiah 40:7—44:30

Gedaliah's Murder and Its Result (40:7—43:7)
Jeremiah Predicts Nebuchadnezzar's Conquest of Egypt (43:8-13)
Jeremiah's Final Message to the Jews in Egypt (44:1-30)

Dated Dialogue (Biographic). Jeremiah 45:1-5

Prophetic Discourses (Biographic). Jeremiah 46:1—51:64

Introduction (46:1)
Concerning Egypt (46:2-26)
Jacob to Be Saved from Afar (46:27-28)
Concerning the Philistines (47:1-7)
Concerning Moab (48:1-47)
Concerning Ammon (49:1-6)
Concerning Edom (49:7-22)
Concerning Damascus (49:23-27)
Concerning Kedar and Hazor (49:28-33)
Concerning Elam (49:34-39)
Concerning Babylon (50:1—51:64)

Historical Appendix (Biographic). Jeremiah 52:1-34

COMMENTARY

PREFACE
Jeremiah 1:1-3

The preface introduces Jeremiah as one of the exiled priests who lived at Anathoth some three miles northeast of Jerusalem. These words also connect Jeremiah's forty-year career as a prophet to three of the last five kings who occupied the throne of David "until the captivity of Jerusalem" in 587 B.C. But the main function of the preface is to sound forth the most distinctive note in the whole book: "The words of Jeremiah . . . to whom the word of the LORD came . . . until . . ."

No book of the Bible illuminates more clearly how and why God converses with man than this Book of Jeremiah. Amid the tumult and clamor of four decades Jeremiah claimed to be hearing the voice of God. He earnestly called upon the people of Judah to hearken unto the divine voice. Wherever one reads in the book he is greeted by the same theme-note with slight variations: "The word of the LORD came to me"; "Thus said the LORD to me"; "The word that came to Jeremiah from the LORD"; "Thus says the LORD."

But does God actually speak to men? The Book of Jeremiah answers with a resounding "Yes." It affirms that God does speak to men ". . . until . . ." The double "until . . . until . . ." is startling. It means that God's word is decisive. God's word rings with finality, because what God says, God does. God speaks to persons. He speaks by persons. He speaks in events. He plucks up and he breaks down. He builds and he plants. This, in short, is the firm, solemn, telling message of the Book of Jeremiah.

EARLIER DISCOURSES (Autobiographic)
Jeremiah 1:4—10:25
Main Topic: Jeremiah Proclaims Judah's Guilt

The discourse form of chapters 1-10 stands apart from the narrative form which distinguishes chapters 11-20. In these discourses the reader is made aware of the major concerns which stirred Jeremiah into action in the earlier stages of his prophetic ministry. But first of all the reader is introduced to Jeremiah himself at the moment of his call and commission as a prophet.

Jeremiah's Call and Commission (1:4-19)

God Calls Jeremiah (1:4-10)

No passage in the Bible describes the interplay between God
and the individual more faithfully than this appealing record of
Jeremiah's call as a prophet. As elsewhere in the Bible, God
speaks: man hears. This time God's word came to a young priest.
The youth hearkened but hesitated. How could he, so young, tell
others what the illuminating word of God had made known to
him? Four active verbs sum up Jeremiah's forthright claim: "Now
the word of the LORD came to me saying, '. . . I formed . . .
knew . . . consecrated . . . appointed you.'" Each verb adds its
own tone to the full call of God to Jeremiah. The verb "formed"
is used here as in Genesis 2:7. God's creative activity is like that
of a potter (compare Jer. 18:1-4), whose handiwork reveals his
design. "Knew" means to have regard for a chosen object (Amos
3:2). "Consecrated" might better be expressed, "separated," as a
vessel is separated (set apart) for a holy use. The Hebrew word
translated "appointed" really means "given" (3:15).

To be formed, chosen, set apart, given by Another: to exist as
a personal self by the deliberate intent of the living God! Here
indeed was food for thought and strength for action. For Jeremiah this moment of divine illumination proved to be a decisive
turning point in his life. A potter takes a newly shaped vessel
from the wheel and says, "Before I formed you I knew you."
These words spoken by the divine Potter meant far more to Jeremiah. He was "set apart" for a distinct work. He was "given" as
a spokesman to the nations. Like an untutored youth Jeremiah
hesitated: "Behold, I do not know how to speak." But the divine
Potter persisted. Symbolically he put forth his hand. This time
he touched Jeremiah's mouth, saying, "Behold, I have put my
words in your mouth." What God had to say to the nations
would surely come to pass. He was about to "pluck up and . . .
break down." He proposed also "to build and to plant." To proclaim his sovereign will to the nations, God had formed Jeremiah
to be a living voice.

How God's Word Came to Jeremiah (1:11-19)

Jeremiah's two visions illustrate *how* God's word first came to
him. Like Amos (1:1; 8:1-2) and Isaiah (2:1), Jeremiah claimed

to "see" what God said. Jeremiah's first vision was reassuring. He saw an "early-awake" tree (vs. 11; the Hebrew word translated "almond" means this). Just as the first tree to put forth a bud betokens the certainty of approaching spring, so God assured Jeremiah that he also was "early awake" over his word. Jeremiah was to speak God's word. God himself would bring it to pass.

The second vision was ominous. The boiling pot symbolized the certainty of judgment "from the north" (vs. 13). The Covenant people had forsaken God. They were worshiping the works of their own hands. Therefore Jerusalem was about to be besieged. The cities of Judah would be invaded. Already a warning sign had appeared. Not long before Jeremiah was called to be a prophet (626 B.C.), Ashurbanipal, the king of Assyria, died. The great Assyrian Empire to the northeast was tottering. The whole Fertile Crescent was in ferment. What power would rise to succeed Assyria? The times indeed were ominous. God was raising up a spokesman to press home his claims upon the Covenant people.

But would God's claims be heeded? Jeremiah now realized that he, too, would be attacked, and by his own stiff-necked generation: kings, princes, priests, people. But God promised to be with him (1:8, 19). Like a fortified city Jeremiah would be kept secure. Like an iron pillar he would be made strong. Like brazen walls he would be able to resist attack.

Jeremiah's Earliest Utterances (2:1—4:4)

There are two distinct features of the utterances recorded in chapters 2 and 3. One of these emphases is the reiterated claim that Jeremiah is speaking for God (repeated some twenty times). The other feature is the significant reference to King Josiah and his reforms. Following the repair of the Temple (622 B.C.) and the finding of the Book of the Law, Jeremiah saw how inadequate were Josiah's attempts at outward reform. Judah had not returned unto God with her whole heart, but only feignedly (3:10). A deeper regeneration of the Covenant people was imperative. The utterances recorded in these chapters may not all have been spoken in the days of Josiah, but all are rightly included here for they all sound the same note.

"My people . . . have forsaken me" (2:1-37)

Jeremiah began by recalling what had made Israel originally

God's chosen people (2:1-3). Like Hosea he depicted their relation to God in terms of the marriage bond. Jeremiah proclaimed that Israel was set apart as a bride to God. But God's people had forgotten their first love (see 2:32 and 3:21), and the gracious gifts of their divine Benefactor: the deliverance from Egypt, guidance through the perilous wilderness, possession of a plentiful land and its goodness. Their leaders who should have sought God's will had failed them (2:4-8).

Figuratively Jeremiah asked his people to look from west to east—from Cyprus to Kedar (an Arabian tribe)—and to consider seriously that no people ever forsakes its ancestral deities lightly. Yet God's people had left the source of their blessings—God, "the fountain of living waters." They had hewed out worthless substitutes, idols, the works of their own hands (1:16), which like broken cisterns could not sustain them (2:9-13). Furthermore, Jeremiah urged Judah to ponder the fate which a century before had overtaken the Kingdom of Israel, whose ruined cities were a timely warning. Had not Egypt and Assyria always despoiled other peoples? It was folly for Judah now to depend upon them rather than upon the Lord her God (2:14-19).

By vivid word pictures Jeremiah showed that Judah had deteriorated. From being a "choice vine," she had become a degenerate plant. Her life was stained with marks like those which lye and soap could not remove. Judah's passion for mates other than her true spouse had led her astray into unrestrained sin. Her thirst for the love of strangers was both futile and fatal. To worship a tree or a stone instead of God was shameful. No such gods would save in time of trouble (2:20-28). Judah should not complain when God corrected his rebellious children. Had he been a wilderness to his people or a land of thick darkness? Could a bride forget her attire? How then could God's people be so faithless to their troth? They had deliberately gone after many lovers. But two of these, Egypt and Assyria, had brought to God's rebellious children only shame. How could they deny their guilt? (2:29-37). Such pointed questions may have stirred the conscience of Jeremiah's generation, yet the will to resist God's claims seemed to be stronger. Therefore Jeremiah followed up his searching questions by forceful entreaties.

"Return, O faithless children" (3:1—4:4)

Following the example of Hosea, Jeremiah likened the ingrained guilt of his people to harlotry. Would they lightly regard the heinousness of their sin, and remain unashamed? Their harlotry had been deliberate, and no language of endearment—"My father, thou art the friend of my youth"—could hide their duplicity, for their ways betrayed them (3:1-5). Jeremiah urged God's case against his people even more strongly by likening Israel to a faithless wife now divorced. The Northern Kingdom had sinned away her day of grace and was now in captivity. But Judah, her treacherous sister, was following Israel's example. Although espousing outward reform under Josiah, Judah was only pretending. This compounded her sin. Yet God wanted faithless Judah to repent. Even faithless Israel might yet be brought home to Zion if she were to acknowledge her guilt (3:6-14).

Jeremiah proclaimed that the Covenant God still yearned over his apostate people to bless rather than to chastise. Guilty Jerusalem could be brought to a pre-eminent place among the nations if God's chastened children would forsake their treacherous ways and turn to him in truth. The voice of weeping and supplication, as of sons who repent of their sin, would be the sign of a genuine return to God their Father. He could then as a divine Physician restore them to health. But their only help was in the very God whom they and their fathers had disobeyed (3:15-25).

God's people would enjoy security, and their example would exert a righteous influence over other nations, only if they would return to God and make their repentance real. But this work must be vital. "Break up your fallow ground," he urged. A foregleam of Jeremiah's vision of the new Covenant is found in his urgent word to circumcise their hearts. Inward cleansing was the only alternative to burning judgment (4:1-4).

The Enemy from the North and the Enemy Within
(4:5—6:30)

Beginning at 4:5 and continuing through chapters 5 and 6, we now find a group of prophecies probably delivered midway in Josiah's reign. They contemplate two different enemies: one is an unidentified enemy "from the north"; the other is Judah's "stubborn and rebellious heart."

The ravages to be wrought by the enemy "from the north" are described in the following passages: 4:5-8; 4:11-31; 5:15-17; 6:1-8; 6:22-26. These passages which describe Judah's enemy "from the north" are cast predominantly in elegiac meter, in which a line of three accents is followed by one of two accents. Although this rhythm cannot always be reproduced in English, the Revised Standard Version has attempted it. The lyric and ecstatic character of these poetic rhapsodies is well suited to Jeremiah's purpose. Here imagination charged with deep emotion is used to stir the "stubborn and rebellious heart" of his listeners. Trumpet blast, anguished cry, death shriek, bitter lamentation, all are used to warn or even to alarm the whole countryside.

Among the various attempts to identify this unnamed enemy "from the north" two may be mentioned: (1) The Scythians, a warlike predatory people from the north, threatened Palestine at this time. But the imagery Jeremiah employs is mixed. The Scythians did not use chariots (compare 4:13 with 5:15-17 and 6:1-6) or siege apparatus. Therefore he could not be referring to the Scythians alone. (2) The Chaldeans invaded Judah later in Jeremiah's career. They did use chariots and besiege cities. Did Jeremiah first speak orally concerning the Scythians, and later on (see ch. 36), when he had put his utterances into written form, did he revise them to bring them up to date? This might account for imagery which could apply to two different enemies. In any case, evil did "loom out of the north" long before Jerusalem fell (4:6; 6:1, 22).

The other enemy described in these chapters is Judah's "stubborn and rebellious heart." This aspect of his people's plight is presented in the following passages: 4:9-10; 5:1-14; 5:18-31; 6:9-21; 6:27-30. How these utterances of Jeremiah came to be arranged to alternate so artistically with those which describe the enemy "from the north" it is difficult to say. Yet as one reads these chapters it becomes clear that the peril of imminent war and invasion is introduced in direct relation to its underlying moral and spiritual causes in Judah.

"I hear ... the alarm of war" (4:5-31)

Jeremiah began these utterances by urging that the trumpet—the alarm signal—be sounded to warn the countryside of imminent danger. Evil from the north was approaching like a destroying lion. Land and city alike were threatened by this instrument of God's fierce anger (4:5-8).

But was the prophet heeded? Apparently not, for other voices were declaring, "It shall be well with you." This prose section

(4:9-10) emphasizes the irony of Jeremiah's task. How could he induce his people to return to God when they relied so readily upon false assurances of security?

The brilliant word pictures which follow exhibit Jeremiah's mental distress, his spiritual anguish, and his overwhelming concern for his people. His references to the "hot wind . . . a wind too full . . . the whirlwind . . ." stress his sense of the grim severity and thoroughness of the coming judgment. His mention of a voice from Dan (north) and the hill country of Ephraim (at the very door of Jerusalem) emphasizes the fact that urgent action was needed if judgment was to be forestalled. In his anguish he discerned that the people were skilled to do evil but not to do good. As he contemplated the fierce anger of God, Jeremiah envisaged a series of cosmic disturbances which resembled the primeval chaos (4:23-28; see Gen. 1:2). The terror-smitten flight of the people before the enemy is made all the more vivid by the prophet's apt description of feminine wiles. All subtle attempts to placate the enemy would be futile. Like a woman in travail the daughter of Zion is pictured as gasping for breath. Her anguish is heard in her death shriek, "Woe is me!" (4:29-31).

"How can I pardon you?" (5:1-14)

Now begins a message in which Jeremiah analyzes the corrupting influences in the life of the nation. God was seeking justice and truth (steadfastness) among his people, but their lives belied the profession of their lips. Adversities had only hardened and embittered them. Jeremiah discovered that the common people and the great men alike had refused to learn the lessons of God's chastenings. Like beasts of burden, which break the yoke and stray away only to fall prey to wild animals, the leaders who had renounced God's ways might expect to encounter consequent judgments. Furthermore Jeremiah found that prosperity had excited the appetite of the people for evil. Their wanton treachery is described in language which attributes to human beings the most lustful animal propensities (5:7-8). Only stern retribution and burning judgment were in store for such a generation, notwithstanding the false prophets whose word would prove to be nothing but wind (5:10-14).

"A nation from afar" (5:15-17)

In a brief but awe-evoking poem Jeremiah continued his description of the "nation from afar" which was to be the instrument of approaching judgment. The unknown tongue, the quiver like an open tomb, the stalwart physique of the soldiery, the cannibal-like treatment of their victims, all might well refer to the Scythians. But the attack on Judah's fortified cities would refer more probably to the Chaldeans as the unnamed enemy. In either case the judgment would be merciless (5:15-17).

"Why has . . . God done all these things to us?" (5:18-31)

Once again Jeremiah pointed to the true cause of the judgment about to overwhelm this foolish and senseless generation. The sea does not pass over its appointed bounds, he observed, but God's people do overpass in deeds of wickedness. Just as God controls the sea and the seasons, so also he can bring judgment on his people for their treachery. Jeremiah laid chief responsibility for the waywardness of the people upon their leaders. Prophet and priest alike were guilty of appalling faithlessness, but the people gave approval, and so sealed their doom (see especially 5:31).

"Evil looms out of the north" (6:1-8)

Once again the enemy out of the north is described by mixed imagery. First the foe is described as a pastoral people (6:3), but later the invader is said to take cities by the use of siege mounds (6:6). The prophet declares that the refugees from Benjamin (north of Jerusalem) will find no security in the Holy City. The enemy is pictured as menacing Tekoa, about twelve miles south of Jerusalem. Beth-haccherem, meaning house of the vineyard, was probably a high point, suitable for signaling, about four and a half miles west of Jerusalem.

"Ask . . . where the good way is; and walk in it" (6:9-21)

Using the figure of a gleaned vineyard, Jeremiah now indicated that the coming judgment would be as thorough as had been the sinning of the people. Israel's captivity was like a first gleaning of the vines. Now it was Judah's turn to be gleaned. "Uncircumcised" ears (vs. 10, margin), means that God's people did not hearken to his claims: "Behold, the word of the LORD is to them an object of scorn." Scorn and covetousness are often linked together in life. Jeremiah protested that the unblushing greed of leaders and people alike could not be eradicated by false protestations of, "Peace, peace," when there was no peace. Rather they were to ask for the ancient paths, the ways that had been proved in actual practice to be good for all people. Only then would they find rest for their souls. But the people stubbornly refused what was good for them. Jeremiah, like Ezekiel, asserted that the prophets were God's appointed watchmen over his people, to keep them in God's ways (Jer. 6:17; Ezek. 3:17; 33:7-9). But the people did not heed. Judah's approaching fall was the fruit of her "devices" (thoughts) and her rejection of the divine law (Torah). For this rejection no sacrifices or religious ceremonies, however costly, could atone.

"Anguish has taken hold of us" (6:22-26)

In keeping with his vision of the boiling pot at the time of his call, Jeremiah asserted again, "Behold, a people is coming from the north country." These ruthless hordes from a distant land were said to be poised for action. The bow, spear, horses, and battle array were all typical of Scythian warfare. The terror and bitter mourning they had produced elsewhere were recalled to stir Judah to repentance. Having failed to respond to the Lord's gentler ministrations through the mouth of his prophet, Judah was warned to be prepared for sterner judgments at the hand of a relentless enemy.

"I have made you an assayer" (6:27-30)

A personal word of God to the prophet about himself concludes the present utterances. It was shown to Jeremiah that it was his function to act as an assayer among God's people. In refining silver, lead was used as an oxidizing agent to carry off the dross. Jeremiah, however, was made to see that the people were so corrupt and stubborn that his assaying work among them was futile. By a play on words the meaning of his early messages is summarized. God's people were like "refuse silver," and so the Lord "refused" them.

The Temple Sermon (7:1—8:3)

A New Situation in Jeremiah's Career

There is an obvious break between the prophecies recorded in chapters 4-6 and those presented in chapters 7-9. The clue to this break is supplied by the experiences of Jeremiah which are recorded in chapter 26. There the occasion of Jeremiah's Temple Sermon early in the reign of Jehoiakim, with its accompanying results, is described. Here (7:1-15) the substance of his stirring message is summarized.

The essence of Jeremiah's Temple Sermon is simply this: a faith which divorces the worship of God from one's obligations to people is no real faith. For fearlessly proclaiming this blunt truth, Jeremiah was put on trial for his life (ch. 26). Here (7:1-15) the words uttered on that occasion are put in greater detail. In fact, the utterances recorded in chapters 7, 8, and 9 all treat various aspects of this same theme. Here, as elsewhere in the Book of Jeremiah, topical treatment rather than precise historical order apparently has determined the present arrangement of the parts.

Jeremiah Preaches in the Temple (7:1-15)

Upon the occasion of some fast, or possibly at the very time of Jehoiakim's enthronement, Jeremiah stood at the gate of one of the Temple courts where many worshipers could hear him. He accused the people of making the Temple a fetish, as though their threefold repetition of the words, "the temple of the LORD" (possibly a current Temple hymn sung by the people), carried with it the potency of a protective charm (7:1-4). Jeremiah insisted that if the people really wanted security and the permanent enjoyment of their good land they should be just to one another and should abstain from oppression. Only so could they satisfy the claims of God upon them as his people. They could not expect feverish devotion to formal worship ("We are delivered!" 7:10) to absolve them from responsibility for the abominations involved in breaking God's commandments or in offering themselves in worship to Baal. "A den of robbers" (7:11) is a place of retreat for thieves between successive acts of plunder. This is what the Covenant people had made of God's house, declared Jeremiah. Jesus quoted these memorable words at his dramatic cleansing of Herod's Temple (Mark 11:17).

Not content merely to plumb the conscience of these vain Temple devotees, Jeremiah gave them a dire warning. God could dispense with the Temple just as he had done with the sanctuary of the Ark at Shiloh many years before. At that time the tribes had taken the Ark from Shiloh into battle as a fetish (I Sam., chs. 4-6). The Ark was captured by the Philistines and the sanctuary at Shiloh was desecrated. The ruins of Shiloh, only eighteen miles north of Jerusalem, may have been a mute but terrible witness to the truth of the prophet's startling words.

Jeremiah Forbidden to Intercede (7:16-20)

As on other occasions (11:14; 14:11-12), Jeremiah was forbidden to pray for this people. Having broken away completely from the recent reforms of Josiah, now, under Jehoiakim, they were supplementing formal Temple ritual by feverish idol worship. Children and parents alike were devoting themselves to the worship of the queen of heaven, a pagan mother goddess. The women of Jerusalem made cakes stamped with her image (see also 44:19). This practice became an abomination in Jerusalem and was one of the contaminating influences which led the nation from bad to worse. Jeremiah warned that the wrath of the Lord would be "poured out on this place."

Jeremiah Condemns the Whole Sacrificial System (7:21-26)

What did Jeremiah mean when he declared, "Thus says the LORD of hosts . . . 'I did not speak to your fathers or command them concerning burnt offerings and sacrifices' "? Was he denying that the Lord had ever instituted sacrifices as a part of the historical relations between himself and his people, or was he strongly affirming their nonessential character? By an emphatic use of rhetorical negation it would appear that he was insisting, as did Amos (5:21-27), that God's fundamental requirement is *obedience*. It is as though he were saying sarcastically: "Do as you please about your sacrifices. They are worthless in the sight of God. It is obedience he wants." Jeremiah was not depreciating the value of sacrifice as such, but was denouncing the current practice of exalting ceremonial into an end in itself. God had placed primal value upon the moral loyalty of their fathers (Deut. 10:12-13). Only as they obeyed God's voice could the people fulfill their part of the Covenant relation. The Hebrew word translated "persistently" (7:13, 25) is a favorite term of Jeremiah's which appears frequently throughout his writings. Sometimes it is used to emphasize that God was *speaking* to his people (7:13; 25:3; 35:14); sometimes that he was *sending* the prophets (7:25; 25:4; 29:19; 35:15; 44:4); or that he was *warning* the people (11:7); or that he was *teaching* them (32:33). This term emphasizes one of the dominant notes in the

book: God is ceaselessly yearning to draw the Covenant people
away from their own destructive devices.

Jeremiah Laments the Rejection of Judah (7:27—8:3)

The apathy and indifference of the sons of Judah to God's
claims drew forth still another stricture from the prophet. Because they had failed to hearken to God's voice or to submit to
correction, Jeremiah saw clearly that "truth" (faithfulness) had
perished among the people as though it were cut off from their
lips. As a sign of mourning the people of Jerusalem were commanded to cut off their hair, for the Lord had rejected "the generation of his wrath." Josiah had destroyed the high place in the
valley of the son of Hinnom, called "Topheth" (II Kings 23), but
now this contaminating high place had been rebuilt as a place of
false worship. Once again sons and daughters might be sacrificed
there to Molech (the pagan god of the Ammonites). By a thun-
derous "Therefore" (7:32), Jeremiah declared that the coming
judgment would be so severe that the name "Topheth" (which
may mean "burning place," Isa. 30:33) would be changed to
"the valley of Slaughter." Where once the people had butchered
their children, they themselves would be butchered, and exposed
to the birds of prey. To be left unburied and exposed (Deut.
28:26) was abhorrent to the Hebrew. The refrain in the last
part of verse 34 is characteristic of the Book of Jeremiah (16:9;
25:10; 33:11), here depicting the desolation of an unhappy land
under judgment. Sterner words are used to conclude Jeremiah's
lament (8:1-3). Not content with slaughter, the enemy is pictured as unearthing the bones of the kings, notables, and other
inhabitants of Jerusalem. He would defile them before the heavenly bodies they had worshiped. The misery of those who escaped
his wrath would be worse than death. If these terrible words shock
the modern ear, what must have been their impact when they
were originally uttered?

Other Timely Utterances (8:4—9:26)

The utterances found in chapters 8 and 9 are all undated and
are only superficially related, since they represent a variety of
circumstances and prophetic moods. Yet it would appear that
they have been incorporated here because they reiterate notes
similar to those already heard in Jeremiah's Temple Sermon.

Jeremiah's most persistent question in these prophecies is "Why?" (8:5, 19, 22; 9:12).

"Why then has this people turned away?" (8:4-7)

Men usually arise when they have fallen, or return to the path when they have strayed. By vivid word pictures Jeremiah accused his people of persisting in error. Into their wayward course they plunged as a horse plunges headlong into battle. Migratory birds like the stork, the turtledove, swallow, and crane obey their natural instincts, but God's people did not obey the law of their being. This Hebrew word translated "ordinance" (8:7) signifies in a comprehensive sense whatever God has ordained or determined, whatever is right according to his ordering. To Jeremiah it seemed incredible that the people could be so unnatural in their relations to their Creator, and he used the best illustrations at his command to emphasize this.

"How can you say, 'We are wise'?" (8:8-22)

Jeremiah accused the religious leaders of Judah of nullifying God's written precepts. The scribes, responsible for interpreting the Law (Torah, or "instruction"), found sanctions for their actions in false interpretations, while the prophets and priests used their positions for greedy gain. Yet without blush of shame such leaders soothed the conscience of the people, saying, "Peace, peace," when there was no peace. Such leaders were likened to sterile grapevines and fig trees, which are good only for fuel. Jeremiah compared his generation to people doomed to perish because they had been given poisoned water to drink.

As though to reinforce the certainty of their doom, Jeremiah pictured the land as invaded by determined horsemen from the extreme north (Dan). He likened the enemy to serpents which could not be charmed. To succumb to such a senseless doom was to Jeremiah sheer folly. Why had his generation provoked its righteous King to anger by persisting in false worship? Was it not as though his people had failed to reap when the harvest was ripe? Or were they not like a person who, stricken with a fatal illness, would refuse the balm of Gilead—a famous healing agent—at the hands of a divine physician?

"O that my head were waters . . . a fountain of tears" (9:1-22)

In the Hebrew Bible, 9:1 is the last verse of chapter 8. It is obvious that the connection between the end of chapter 8 and the beginning of chapter 9 is very close. Oppressed with deepest melancholy, Jeremiah lamented his spiritual isolation. When he thought of the certain doom awaiting his generation he could weep day and night. As he viewed the treachery and infidelity all about him he yearned to be utterly separated from his people in some lodging place in the wilderness; he lamented that every man was a Jacob (supplanter). Every neighbor was unbrotherly. Adultery, deceit, slander, lying, were the most common sins among his neighbors. Such sins were clear proof that these people did not know the Lord. Yet Jeremiah knew that he could never really abandon his people, for he was their appointed refiner and tester. Added to everything else he had said, Jeremiah now pictured the weeping and wailing for the desolation in the land, the flight of birds and beasts, as an indication of Judah's coming ruin and exile. Such signs should be enough, thought Jeremiah, to make a wise man understand God's ways.

Where will one find a more vivid or more moving image of impending doom than Jeremiah's picture of death as a "reaper" in his elegy of 9:17-22? Professional mourners customarily were employed at funerals to make loud lamentations. Now no such conventional dirges would do. These professional mourners were urged to teach real laments to their daughters and their neighbors, for death was about to reap a grim harvest.

"Let him who glories glory in this" (9:23-24)

To glorify God is to exhibit his character in thought, word, or deed. The men of Jeremiah's generation, like those of every age, had their own scale of values: human wisdom (culture), military might (technical skill), material wealth (economic plenty). It makes very little difference how men change the emphasis; from age to age men are shown to be the same self-willed creatures: boastful of wisdom, trustful in might, lustful for riches. Thus they blind themselves to the eternal and transcendent character of that glorious Being who delights to practice kindness, to exercise justice, and to do righteousness in the earth.

"Circumcised but yet uncircumcised" (9:25-26)

By what more appropriate figure could the essence of Jeremiah's Temple Sermon (7:1-15) be set forth than by the one used here? Whatever obscures men's vision of God and his ways, whatever beclouds their sense of duty to their fellow men, must in the end be swept away. Whether the obsession be the Temple (or Shiloh), the sacrifices or formal worship, external rites like circumcision, or even the word of the sages, God could and would dispense with all these accessories. He would send into captivity the men of this generation who were substituting empty forms for real worship, individual mysticism for public responsibility. Jeremiah's people who practiced circumcision were in fact uncircumcised! All men—whether they lived in Egypt, Judah, Edom, Ammon, Moab, or in the desert—all who failed to recognize the claims of the God who exercises kindness, justice, and righteousness in the earth, were in truth "uncircumcised in heart."

The Living God and the Impotent Idols (10:1-16)

Jeremiah 10:1-16 presents a variety of textual and linguistic difficulties to the interpreter. These verses interrupt the sequence between the close of chapter 9 and 10:17-25 as though they had been inserted here arbitrarily. The Greek translation (the Septuagint) omits 10:6-8, 10, and part of 10:16. The same translation inserts 10:9 after the first sentence of 10:5. The Revised Standard Version indicates in the margin that 10:11 is written in Aramaic prose. Moreover, 10:12-16 is repeated in 51:15-19. This passage, by virtue of its position and its textual complexities, is a puzzle. As a whole the utterance reminds the reader more of such passages as Isaiah 40:19-20; 44:9-20; and 46:5-7 than of Jeremiah. Here, as in the passages in Isaiah, the exiled people of God, surrounded by idolatry, are urged not to adopt the practices of their heathen neighbors but to adhere to the worship of the one true God.

Two perils of the heathen environment surrounding the exiled Hebrews are pointed out: pagan interpretations of heavenly portents which inspire terror, and the manufacture of idols which tend to materialize worship. The prophet pours scorn upon the impotence of idols, the work of men's hands. They must be carried because there is no life in them; nor can they do either evil or good. However precious the material of which they are made, or however attractive their ornamentation, they are only the work of skillful men (10:1-10).

At 10:11 the sequence of thought is broken by the sentence written in Aramaic prose. This sentence may be an early addition to the text. In its present position the sentence would appear to be a suggestion made by a prophet to the Hebrews in exile, giving the Covenant people a response to make whenever they are invited to join in idol worship.

Like Isaiah 40:12-17, the prophetic words of 10:12-16 offer a vivid description of the creative activity and wisdom of the Lord of Hosts (see also Jer. 51:15-19). They proclaim that the wise and powerful Creator of the world is the abiding portion of Jacob (the Covenant people). The one who has formed all things, the Lord of Hosts, is sovereign over all that he has made.

Other Timely Utterances, Continued (10:17-25)

The remainder of chapter 10 (vss. 17-25) continues the discourse which was interrupted at 9:26, by pointing to an imminent exile (10:17-22). It is concluded by a prayer for personal correction (10:23-24), united with one which yearns for retribution upon Judah's enemies (10:25).

"Behold, I am slinging out the inhabitants" (10:17-22)

The prophet is now represented as carrying on an imaginary conversation with a personified Jerusalem. The besieged city is reminded that the time of mourning is over (compare 9:17-22). Therefore the women may well take up their bundles from the ground and begin the long trek into captivity, for the Lord is slinging his people out of their land (10:17-18). The words spoken in 10:19-22 are uttered in the first person, and it is difficult to know whether the prophet is speaking for himself or is personifying the nation. The expressions "My hurt . . . my wound . . . this is an affliction, and I must bear it . . ." might lead one to conclude that Jeremiah is describing his own pain over the fate of his people. However, the succeeding metaphors, "My tent [compare 4:20] . . . my children . . . my curtains . . . the shepherds . . . ," all suggest that by these terms Jeremiah means to express the anticipated hurt of the exiles. Jerusalem, the mother city, is pictured as lamenting that her land has been despoiled and her children dispersed. She mourns because her shepherds (leaders) have been too stupid to gather in her scattered flock. Rumor has become startling fact. A great commotion out of the north country indicates that the desolation of the cities of Judah is about to begin.

"Correct me, O Lord, but in just measure." (10:23-24)

Among the choicest words of Jeremiah are those which record his conversations with God. Some of them, like this one, are hardly more than ejaculations (for example, 15:11; 20:13), yet taken together with his longer prayers (for example, 20:7-18; 32:17-25) these sentence prayers indicate how steady and deep the stream of Jeremiah's communion with God really flowed. These interchanges with God show also why Jeremiah has been called "the father of true prayer." Here Jeremiah recognizes that "the way of man is not in himself"; that is to say, he belongs to Another. When a man fails to acknowledge this relationship and acts as though he were self-sufficient, his knowledge of himself becomes perverted—"It is not in man who walks to direct his steps"—and so he requires divine correction. But Jeremiah pleads that God may be merciful. So desperate is his state that justice alone would destroy him utterly.

"Pour out thy wrath" (10:25)

The strong words of 10:25 which invoke God's wrath upon the nations that "have devoured Jacob" are parallel to and almost identical with the words of the psalmist in Psalm 79:6-7. This verse may well be regarded as belonging to utterances which had accumulated "around Jeremiah," rather than from those which were authentically "by Jeremiah" himself.

NARRATIVES AND PRONOUNCEMENTS
(Autobiographic)
Jeremiah 11:1—20:18

Main Topics: Jeremiah's Confessions and Judah's Approaching Doom

The beginning of a new section in the composition of the book is observable here, where the discourse form (chapters 1-10) shifts to predominantly narrative treatment. Interwoven with the narration of personal experiences of Jeremiah are severe pronouncements of judgment upon Judah.

The Words of the Covenant (11:1—12:17)

The discovery of the Book of the Law (622 B.C.) was a significant turning point in the reign of Josiah (II Kings 22:8-20).
We are not told expressly what Jeremiah did after this event.
But in chapters 11 and 12 we may find some illuminating clues
to the prophet's activities at that moment. For instance, Jeremiah
was urged to speak in the cities of Judah and on the streets of
Jerusalem (11:2, 6). His references to "this covenant" (11:2,
3, 6) correspond to statements concerning the Covenant in Deuteronomy 29:1, 9, 14, 21. His use of "cursed" (11:3) and
"Amen" ("So be it"—11:5) correspond to the similar terms
repeated in Deuteronomy 27:5-26. These striking similarities
suggest that the Covenant mentioned in Deuteronomy was the
very one to which Jeremiah advocated adherence. The people
resisted his efforts (11:9-13), but Jeremiah cross-examined their
evil practices even more thoroughly (11:14-17). He now discovered to his grief that his own people at Anathoth were plotting to destroy him (11:18-23), whereupon he carried his personal distress to God in prayer (12:1-4), and in turn received
a bold, searching answer (12:5-6). This, it would appear, is the
topical sequence intended by the arrangement of the successive
parts in 11:1—12:6.

If the reactions to the prophet's preaching recorded in 11:9-17
belong to Jehoiakim's reign rather than to Josiah's, as some
maintain, it would in no way lessen the import of Jeremiah's
mission to his people as reported here. No passage in the Bible
represents a more powerful or significant retrospect of a man
under stress because he has dared to say "Amen" to God.

The lament of 12:7-13 and the warning recorded in 12:14-17
doubtless refer to situations in the life of the prophet other than
those related in the words of 11:1—12:6, but the overtones of
Jeremiah's crisis are heard ringing both in the lament of verses
7-13 and in the warning of verses 14-17, as a closer analysis of
chapters 11 and 12 reveals.

Reactions in Judah and Jerusalem (11:1-17)

Is it not entirely in keeping with his call that the young prophet
should have identified himself with the reforms of Josiah? Living
close to the people as he did (5:1, 31; 11:6, 9), would he not

have been among the first to feel the recoil against these reforms? Old customs die hard in agricultural communities. Although we are told in II Kings 23:3 that "all the people joined in [stood to] the covenant," this need not mean any more than that they gave outward assent to it because they were required at the king's command to do so.

Jeremiah's reference to the "iron furnace" (11:4) recalls Deuteronomy 4:20 (see also I Kings 8:51), which stresses God's gracious deliverance of Israel from Egypt. God's mighty act in redeeming his enslaved people is cited as a motive for listening to his voice and for keeping his Covenant. Furthermore, by referring to a "land flowing with milk and honey," Jeremiah reminded his generation of the bountiful promises made to the fathers (Deut. 6:3; 11:9; 26:9), which God had kept "as at this day."

As the twelve tribes at Ebal and Gerizim were to give assent by saying "Amen" to the curses and blessings pronounced by the Covenant (Deut. 27:11-26), so Jeremiah would have his own people assent. As for himself, the prophet is said to have pledged personal adherence to the Covenant: "Then I answered, 'So be it, LORD' " (11:5). To support God's claims upon the people of Judah even more strongly, Jeremiah emphasized the solemn warnings God had given to their fathers, which they, to their own hurt, had stubbornly resisted (11:6-8).

The "revolt among the men of Judah and the inhabitants of Jerusalem" might refer to local uprisings or, possibly, to quiet but determined resistance to the reforms across the land. Whether this subversive movement took place in the times of Josiah or during the reign of Jehoiakim, Jeremiah saw clearly that Josiah's reforms had not changed the heart of the Covenant people. They were still intent on burning incense to other gods. An impenitent people might expect help neither from the true God nor from their impotent idols (11:9-13).

Even Jeremiah's intercessions, he was reminded, would be unavailing so long as the people merely desired relief from their troubles without repenting of their ways. The Hebrew text of 11:15 is obscure, but the Revised Standard Version rightly adopts the reading of the Greek text here, which admirably suits the context. Jeremiah's meaning is clear. He asked why the Covenant people had come to God's house, since their deeds were so vile. He saw that no offering, however costly, could ever be a substitute for wholehearted dedication. Furthermore, Judah might be like a luxuriant olive tree, but God would consume it even though he himself had planted it.

Reactions at Anathoth (11:18-23)

The priests of Anathoth were the descendants of Abiathar, who had been exiled there by Solomon for participation in the insurrection of Adonijah (I Kings 2:26-27). Since that time the sons of Zadok had performed the priestly functions in Jerusalem. Josiah's reforms, which tended to centralize all worship in Jerusalem and to prohibit it elsewhere (II Kings 23:4-20), entrenched the sons of Zadok more firmly in Jerusalem, and so the Anathoth priests were excluded even more fully than before. May it not be that this is what stirred the men of Anathoth into a frenzy of hate when one of their own number, by prophesying in the name of the Lord, lent his support to the reforms of Josiah? But Jeremiah confessed that he was like a gentle lamb led to the slaughter. He was now to learn the bitterness of being an enemy in his own household. His first impulse was to resent this treachery on the part of his own people and to pray for vengeance upon them. His discernment that a terrible fate was in store for those who persecuted him proved to be only a temporary resolution of his problem. Now Jeremiah was compelled not only to face the rectitude of God's ways but also to determine what his own future course of action was to be.

Reactions of Jeremiah (12:1-6)

Under deep stress Jeremiah revealed the bitter depths of his struggle. The prosperity of the wicked has always perplexed men of God. Typical examples which parallel Jeremiah's experience are those found in Job 21 and Psalms 37 and 73. Hitherto Jeremiah had accepted, apparently without question, the righteousness of God. The conscious integrity of his own motives only made his suffering at this time all the more poignant.

Before he could pursue his prophetic task any further, the prophet was compelled to think through the very foundations of his faith. And so it came to pass that each factor that made up his urgent problem passed in turn before his gaze: God, the wicked, Jeremiah, the wicked, God! The reader of these tense words can trace each succeeding level through which the prophet's mind descended until he touched bottom. He began by reaffirming his confidence in God the righteous One. Yet this unshakable conviction threw into even bolder relief the prosperity of the wicked, whose perfidy in turn greatly magnified in Jeremiah's consciousness the purity of his own intentions (12:3). In one breath Jeremiah justified himself; in the next he turned vindictively upon the wicked. "How long," he inquired, "how long will God tolerate such men?" Jeremiah had indeed touched bottom. Was he thenceforth to live in a sink of bitterness? Or would he rise to the higher level which his mission required?

Now comes the searching question of the righteous God in 12:5. If Jeremiah failed now, what would he do when things got much worse? If he stumbled in a safe land (his hometown at Anathoth?), what might he expect to do in the lion-infested jungles of Jordan (his coming trials in Jerusalem)? This is hardly the kind of comfort a man in deep trouble might expect: "Cheer up, the worst is yet to come!" God did not disparage Jeremiah's hurt: his kinsmen have indeed dealt treacherously with him. But still Jeremiah was summoned to heroic action. There was no need for him to sulk in bitterness.

Reactions of Judah's Neighbors (12:7-13)

Although the words recorded in 12:7-13 probably refer to a situation other than that just described, the poem is not inappropriately placed here in topical sequence. One need but compare the metaphors of the two passages to observe their striking similarities. Jeremiah's household had dealt treacherously with him. Was it the taste of this bitter cup that enabled him now to envisage how God's household was treating God? "I have forsaken my house, I have abandoned my heritage": how could God's pain over his people and pity for his heritage be more poignantly expressed? God is represented here as posing a blunt question: "Is my heritage to me like a speckled bird of prey?" As a bird of variegated plumage is attacked by birds of prey, as an unprotected vineyard is trampled by ruthless shepherds, so Judah had unwittingly invited predatory attacks upon herself by abandoning God. And so God's "pleasant portion" had been despoiled.

Restoration of Judah's Neighbors (12:14-17)

At the time of his call Jeremiah had been appointed to be a prophet unto the nations. He had also been reminded that God was at work among the nations "to pluck up and . . . to build" (1:10). This brief but undated utterance emphasizes the international scope of Jeremiah's message. For him God's sovereignty extended far beyond the bounds of his own people. Here it is affirmed that even Judah's evil neighbors could be incorporated among the Covenant people were they to abandon the ways of Baal and to swear by the name of the Lord. Instead of being plucked up from their land they should be "built up in the midst of my people."

The Linen Waistcloth Episode (13:1-11)

This strange episode has been interpreted both as a parable and as a vision. In either case the story would have no foundation in fact but would have been told with a purely didactic end in view. But could it have been an actual experience? There are those who thus explain the passage by translating the Hebrew word *Perath* or *Parah* (here translated "Euphrates," as elsewhere in Jeremiah; for example, 46:2) with a change of one letter from *Parah* to *Farah*. This place (Farah) is about five and one-half miles northeast of Jerusalem near Anathoth (Joshua 18:23) and is identified today as *Khirbet el-Farah*. Such an explanation is in keeping with the environs of Farah, with its flowing stream and fissured rock. In this case the journey required of Jeremiah would have been very short. On the other hand, the episode may be regarded as part of an actual journey to the Euphrates made when Jeremiah was in flight from King Jehoiakim. After the fifth year of Jehoiakim (36:9-32), Jeremiah was compelled to hide, with Baruch, after the writing of the first scroll. Where would the prophet and his scribe have been secure? Hardly in Jerusalem, or nearby Anathoth. Certainly not in Egypt, considering what had happened to Uriah (26:20-23). Furthermore, Jeremiah was known by Chaldean officers (39:11-14). May it not have been that Jeremiah actually was in Babylon during the latter years of Jehoiakim's reign? If so, when he returned to Jerusalem upon Jehoiakim's death and just before Jehoiachin's captivity (13:18-19), he could appropriately have related this bit of experience and followed it up with its impressive moral.

The symbolic act, as explained by the prophet (13:8-11), illustrates the general truth that everything useful has a function.

The function of a waistcloth is to cleave to the loins of the wearer. Just so the glory of Judah was to cleave to the Lord. The waist-cloth became spoiled when it was hidden in a cleft of the rock (13:4-7). So also proud Judah was spoiled by stubborn devotion to false gods. God had bound Judah to himself in sacred covenantal relation. But by cleaving to others rather than to the Lord, Judah had become spoiled and was now good for nothing!

Additional Messages (13:12-27)

"Every jar shall be filled with wine" (13:12-14)

Sooner or later every outdoor preacher gets heckled by the crowd. One can sense the pique of the crowd to whom Jeremiah was speaking when he declared the commonplace truth that "Every jar shall be filled with wine." Of course they all knew that! It has been suggested that the reply was voiced by some toper in the audience. The words of the text literally translated should read, "We know, of course, don't we, that every jar will be filled with wine?" "Yes," bluntly rejoined Jeremiah, "just as empty storage jars [some might well have been standing close by] are destined to be filled with wine, so also the men of Judah are to be filled with horror ["drunkenness"] during the coming crisis." Reeling helplessly as drunken sots, one against another, they all would surely perish.

"Hear and give ear; be not proud" (13:15-27)

One can gather from certain suggestive details, as well as from the wider context, in what a pathetic, if not desperate, situation these wistful warning lines were produced. Upon his death King Jehoiakim had bequeathed a dangerous situation to his widow Nehushta and his eighteen-year-old son Jehoiachin. During the last five years of his troubled reign Jehoiakim had brazenly rebelled against Nebuchadnezzar (II Kings 24:1-7). Meanwhile, until the time had come to take proper measures, Nebuchadnezzar plagued Jehoiakim with predatory bands of neighboring tribesmen. Now the day of reckoning was approaching. Jeremiah had given timely warnings to Jehoiakim for his folly and perfidy (see 22:13-19). He knew that the day of evil was at hand. He clung resolutely, nevertheless, to a deeply cherished hope that some element of good in his people might assert itself.

Twilight was indeed descending upon Judah. As a traveler

turns in for the night, lest his feet stumble and he be compelled
to wander in deep darkness in a strange land, Judah was urged
to turn and give glory to the Lord her God (13:16). Boldly
addressing the king and the queen mother, the prophet urged
them to humble themselves (13:18). Let them expect no inter-
vention from the south at the last moment. It was from the
north that the relentless scatterer of God's flock was about to
come. Jeremiah asked them to consider what to say to enemies
who should have been their friends. Had Judah grown so accustomed to doing evil that she had lost the ability to change her
way? Can the Ethiopian change his skin or the leopard his spots?
Would that Jerusalem would still cast her lot with God and be
made clean! (vs. 27). Her lot, however, was to be scattered like
chaff driven by the wind from the desert. In 597 B.C. the king
and the queen mother and ten thousand of the best people of
the land were taken into captivity by Nebuchadnezzar (II Kings
24:8-17). The fall of Jerusalem was yet to be delayed for eleven
years, but darkness was already descending upon Judah.

Judah's Doom and the Prophet's Anguish (14:1—15:21)

Chapters 14-20 present messages of Jeremiah delivered upon
various occasions. They are all undated. Interwoven with these
prophecies are a number of autobiographical sketches known as
"Jeremiah's Confessions," which illustrate the prophet's mounting despair over his vocation, his sense of isolation and loneliness, and his physical and mental anguish under persecution.
Here, as elsewhere in the present structure of the book, topical
arrangement has prevailed over strict historical order. Included
are passages which probably came from materials about Jeremiah rather than by Jeremiah himself (for example, 17:19-27).

Judah During the Drought (14:1—15:4)

One of the first difficulties encountered by the reader of this
passage is to discern who is speaking. As in other prophetic
books (for example, Isaiah, Micah, Habakkuk), Jeremiah's
prophecies occasionally are cast into dramatic dialogue, and this
certainly is the case here, where the speaker changes as part
succeeds part: the title (14:1); the setting (vss. 2-6); the speech
of the people (vss. 7-9); the reply of the prophet (vs. 10); the
conversation of the Lord and the prophet (vss. 11-16); the ad-

JEREMIAH 14:1—15:4   **51**

dress of the prophet to the people (vss. 17-18); the plea of the
people (vss. 19-22); the answer of the Lord to the people (15:
1-4).

The situation pictured in the setting is one of severe drought
in Judah. There is no water (vs. 3), no rain (vs. 4), no grass
(vs. 5), and no herbage (vs. 6). In the city as well as in the field,
nobleman and servant, plowman and beast, suffer alike. The
people sit in the shade of a city gate in deep mourning, pleading
for deliverance (vs. 2).

The pronouns of 14:7-9 are all in the plural. Three interpretations are possible. Is this an indication that the people are urgently interceding for themselves? Is the prophet confessing his
people's waywardness but pleading God's mercy as their hope
and stay? (14:8-9). Or are these words of the prophet spoken to
probe the hollow pretensions which he hears the people making
at the gate? The passage has been interpreted in all three ways.
But from the following words attributed to the Lord (14:10) it
would appear that the latter view is in keeping with the context,
for the petitions of the people, whatever their motive, are denied.
A paraphrase of the passage thus far traces the progress of
thought as follows: Your present physical drought is but a parable of your true moral condition. Your empty cisterns (14:3)
are like your empty lives. You say, "Our iniquities testify against
us, our backslidings are many, and we have sinned against thee,
O LORD." This is startlingly true. But why do you go on sinning?
Why do you continue backsliding? You have not restrained your
feet (14:10). Instead you lay the source of your troubles on
God. You call him the hope of Israel, your savior in the time of
trouble, yet at the same time you charge him with indifference
to your needs. You imply his impotence to help you, as though
he were no more available than a stranger or a wayfarer, or as
though he were confused like a stunned man. Then you brazenly
declare: "We are called by your name. Save us and thus redeem
your reputation!"

This view is substantiated by the conversation between the
Lord and the prophet (14:11-16), which may be restated as
follows: No! God cannot accept his people on such terms. He
can only let their iniquities bring their own reward upon them.
Do they think that fasting and sacrifices will do them any good,
when their minds and hearts are set on continuing their per-
versity? Sword, famine, pestilence, will consume them. Have the

prophets declared that there is no such danger? Then it must be said that these men prophesy lies, and to act upon their word is only to accept the unhappy consequences which assuredly will follow. The prophets as well as their victims will be consumed.

Jeremiah's pain for his people and their woes is expressed in a lament (14:17-19) very much like those uttered upon other occasions (for example, 8:18—9:1; 13:17). Here he is pained even more by the fact that the people have been deceived by their supposed spiritual leaders (prophets and priests) who "ply their trade through the land" at the people's expense, and who show that they have no true experience of God and his ways.

The dramatic sequence of this passage is continued by the interjection of still another impassioned plea on the part of the people, and an even more determined rejection of them on the part of God (14:19—15:4). The intent of this plea and its rejection may be paraphrased as follows: You rightly acknowledge your own wickedness and the iniquities of your fathers. But will you question God's goodness by asking, "Have you utterly rejected Judah, and does your soul loathe Zion?" You ask why God has smitten you instead of sending peace. Will you remind him of his Covenant with you when by your acts you have repudiated your relation to him? Would you put God to the test as though you were urging him to prove his power and bring the drought to an end by sending rain? No! there is no hope for such a people. Even if Moses and Samuel interceded for you, under such conditions no mercy could be shown you. Instead, four destroyers—sword, dogs, birds of prey, and beasts of earth —will be sent to devour you. The deeds and days of Manasseh are being repeated.

Judah's Winnowing and Jeremiah's Woes (15:5-21)

As with other prophecies in this section (chs. 14-20), there is no way of knowing at what precise moment in his career the prophet spoke these stirring words (15:5-21). The two features of his tension, however, are clear. Jeremiah bewails the futile chastenings of the Covenant people (15:5-9); with mixed emotions he contemplates his own woes and receives the Lord's answer (15:10-21).

Jeremiah remonstrates first with Jerusalem: Who will be concerned about your welfare? You keep on going backward by persistently rejecting God's claims. God is weary with relenting. (For the meaning of the word "relent" or "repent" see comment on 18:8-10.) Although God has sent chastening disciplines, you have not heeded. He has stretched out his hand against you. He has winnowed you. He has bereaved you. Even so you have not turned from your ways.

At this point Jeremiah's imagery becomes even more particular and pathetic: Widows have been mutiplied. Young mothers have been taken. Anguish, terror, shame, disgrace, death! These mounting disasters, the lot of the Covenant people, were declared by the prophet to be the fatal consequences of their apostasy.

Among the confessions of Jeremiah, the following passage is one of the most poignant unveilings of his whole inner life (15:10-21). Jeremiah's stern messages, like the preceding example for instance, had evoked severe reactions and contentions among the people. His stinging attacks upon their sins and his relentless probings of their hardness and indifference to God's claims could only have made them bitter. Jeremiah was made to feel that his fate was as bad as that of a maligned moneylender. The Hebrew text of 15:11-12 is obscure, and the English translations depend upon emendation or conjecture to give the sense. The prophet may mean that even these testing experiences were not without profit: "So let it be, O LORD!" Jeremiah was convinced that he had sought only the good of his enemies, for he had pleaded for them in the time of their trouble. (On other occasions he made a similar plea; see 17:16; 18:20.) Yet he wondered whether his strength alone could break their power. (The best iron and bronze came from the north.) How could he in his own strength resist the hardness of those to whom he must proclaim God's word? (15:13-14 is parallel to 17:3-4, where the message is given an appropriate setting.)

Jeremiah had suffered reproach from his enemies and longed to be avenged. Yet he had a sure source of comfort. God's words had been a satisfying joy to his heart. Like Ezekiel (2:8—3:3) Jeremiah is represented as eating God's words. And like the Seer on Patmos centuries later (Rev. 10:8-10), Jeremiah found God's words to be both bitter and sweet. It is not so strange, therefore, to find the prophet giving expression to two quite widely contrasted moods. The word of the Lord came to him indeed. With it came not only pain and sorrow but sometimes also joy and gladness (15:15-16).

The prophetic vocation had isolated Jeremiah from the common human satisfactions he rightfully craved. The terrible doom hovering over his people intensified his personal loneliness. It would seem, in fact, that his sufferings would never cease, like a wound that refused to be healed. His bitter words in verses 17 and 18 need no comment, they speak for themselves. Such strong language reveals how intimate Jeremiah's communion with God really was. It is good for a man to bare his soul to God alone, yet, even so, one who speaks such words as these must undergo a radical change if he would continue to be God's mouthpiece. The Lord therefore called upon Jeremiah to repent, and do his first works (vs. 19). His words had approached blasphemy, but the Lord understood. Upon repentance Jeremiah could stand before God, that is, be his servant or minister. Once again he could utter "what is precious, and not what is worthless." Once again he could act as God's voice to God's people. Then, the Lord repeated the promise made to Jeremiah at the first (vs. 20; see 1:18-19).

Miscellaneous Experiences and Utterances (16:1—17:27)

Chapters 16 and 17 are a striking example of the "patchwork" construction of this book which puzzles all readers and interpreters. Here the reader is presented with a series of miscellaneous personal experiences and prophetic utterances which correspond to the major topical interest of chapters 14-20. The personal experiences (autobiographic) emphasize the prophet's loneliness. The prophetic utterances sound the note of Judah's impending judgment.

The loose connection of the parts is indicated, for example, by the manner in which 16:14-15 (which is parallel to 23:7-8, where these words have an appropriate relation to what precedes) interrupts the progress of thought. In fact, the paragraph on the hunters and fishers (16:16-18) is the true sequel of 16: 10-13, for it recites in grim particulars how God will fish and hunt for the guilty men of Judah whose sins are depicted there in such strong terms.

Jeremiah's Personal Loneliness (16:1-9)

In a graphic way the meaning of Jeremiah's solitary life as an object lesson to his people is pictured. The denial of a home of his own, and his call to a life uncheered by wife or children, would serve as a sign that all homes of his land were under impending doom, that deaths from disease, sword, and famine were on the way. Jeremiah tells how he was forbidden to enter the house of mourning, as a sign that God had withdrawn his mercies from the nation. Great and small alike would lie unburied and unlamented. To cut or make oneself bald for the dead had been prohibited in Deuteronomy (Deut. 14:1), but it seems to have become a current practice (Jer. 41:4-5). The coming judgment would be so severe that even this practice would not be performed. Neither would the conventional practices of breaking bread for the mourner or of giving him the cup of consolation be possible. Furthermore, Jeremiah was denied the common joys of friendly intercourse, such as entering the house of feasting. This was to be a sign that these joys also were to be withdrawn from his people.

The Meaning of Judah's Fate (16:10-21)

When the people would ask the prophet why such severe judgments were being meted out to them, he was to reply: Their fathers had worshiped false gods, but this generation had sinned worse than their fathers by stubbornly refusing to heed God's warnings. Therefore God was proposing to hurl them out of their land. This stern answer is made still more emphatic by the picture of the fishers and hunters (16:16-18). God would thoroughly chasten his people, and none could escape. He would search them out as diligently as they had polluted his land with detestable idols.

But this stern message is tempered by the prophet's knowledge of God's everlasting mercy. A new "exodus" was promised to his disciplined people. God's judgments in the end would be vindicated. Just as the fathers had been delivered from their slavery in Egypt, so also the chastened people would be brought back by God to their own land again (vss. 14-15).

The vindication of God's severity is now illustrated in a further way (16:19-20). Relying upon the authenticity of his divine call (1:18-19), Jeremiah envisions the way in which the nations of the earth would turn from their vain idol worship to seek God's blessing. The judgments of God thus would be vindicated. The nations would know indeed that his name is the Lord (16:21). Other prophets also looked for the vindication of God's holy name among the peoples (see, for example, Ezek. 36:23; Isa. 59:18-19).

Typical Observations and Sayings (17:1-27)

Chapter 17 is a collection of observations and sayings which, as they are now arranged, have no organic unity. They nevertheless aptly present, by a variety of forms, examples of prophetic preaching: An Indictment of Judah's Guilt (vss. 1-4); A Psalm (vss. 5-8); Two Proverbs (vss. 9-10, and 11); An Invocation (vss. 12-13); A Prayer (vss. 14-18); and A Sabbath Proclamation (vss. 19-27).

Judah's guilt is illustrated by an example drawn from the engraver's art (17:1-4). Accordingly it is said that the deep set of Judah's heart-guilt could no more be eradicated than could marks engraved upon rock by an iron stylus or a diamond point (compare Job 19:24). The Hebrew text of verse 2 is difficult to interpret. In this context it may mean that the guilt of Judah was so deeply ingrained that it would be remembered by all future generations. Meanwhile guilty Judah and her treasures— the gift of God's bounty (her "heritage")—would be despoiled. Exiled from her own land to a foreign country, Judah would there be compelled to serve her enemies.

The reader recognizes at once the striking similarity between the poem in 17:5-8 and Psalm 1. As an introduction to the Psalter the First Psalm describes the man whose delight is in the Law (instruction) of the Lord, in contrast to the one who walks in the counsel of the wicked. In Jeremiah both the form and the stress of the poetry are more elevated than in Psalm 1. In the first place, the fundamental contrast is sharper. The desert shrub, in a parched wilderness, barely manages to eke out a miserable existence. The riverside tree whose roots are watered by the living stream flourishes through heat and drought. In the second place, the stress of this poem is more striking than that of Psalm 1. Here the fruitage (outcome) of a man's rootage (commitment) is more brilliantly expressed. The one does not "see" any good come to pass. His domain is in an uninhabited saltland. The other is like a well-watered tree. He is not anxious amid drought. His "leaves remain green" and he does not cease from bearing fruit.

To grasp the meaning of the proverb of the deceitful heart (vss. 9-10), it is necessary to discriminate carefully between the

terms used. The Hebrews symbolized the various activities of
the inner life as located in certain physical organs. For instance,
the kidneys were regarded as the seat of the innermost emotions.
The heart was thought to be the organ of the reason and in-
telligence, or even the will. There are four passages in Jeremiah,
including this one, where both of these terms are used to refer
to the inner life of man. The others are 11:20; 12:2-3; and
20:12. The translation of 17:9-10 as found in the Revised
Standard Version does not bring out adequately the essential
distinction between these terms. It might be clearer if it read
instead:

> The heart is deceitful above all things,
>   and exceedingly weak;
>   who can know it?
> I the LORD search the heart
>   and try the reins (kidneys) . . .

What did Jeremiah mean by employing both terms to describe
the activities of the inner life? Something indeed is desperately
wrong about man, and Jeremiah with all the skill of a physician
was pointing precisely to the source of man's illness as well as
to the One who can bring healing. It is as though he were saying:
"I, the LORD, take account of a man's thoughts and affections,"
or, better yet, "I, the LORD, am continually searching out a man's
deepest thoughts and testing his yearnings."

Using a popular belief that the partridge is forsaken by her
brood, the prophet, in another proverb, emphasizes the insecurity
of ill-gotten gain (vs. 11). Whether he had any particular individual in mind or not is difficult to say. On one occasion Jeremiah charged Jehoiakim with having eyes and heart only for
dishonest gain (22:13-19). On the other hand, if Jeremiah had
no specific individual in mind he might well have been thinking
of Judah who, during the years, had been gathering a brood of
falsehoods (see 5:30-31).

Those who are content to interpret the gracious words of
verses 12 and 13 merely as an affirmation of the greatness of
the Temple fail to place proper value on the word translated
"sanctuary." A temple may be a sanctuary, but not every sanctuary is a temple. As used in this passage, "sanctuary" is more
than a place of worship; it is safety, refuge, security (see Deut.

19:4-10; I Kings 1:50). Here God's gracious throne, a symbol
of his sovereign authority over all life, is affirmed to be a man's
security amid all peril.

When translated as an invocation addressed to "The Hope of
Israel" these exalted words may be read: "O Lord, throne of
glory, exalted from the beginning, the place of our sanctuary,
hope of Israel, all who forsake thee shall be put to shame . . ."
In short, God's glorious omnipotence is said to be the hope of
Israel! The exercise of his divine authority over Israel was like
a benediction of peace upon the Covenant people. But to deny
that authority was to forsake the fountain of living waters (compare 2:13). Israel was not to find security by seeking sanctuary.
Israel would enjoy sanctuary only by maintaining right relations
to God's glorious throne.

No one could speak as plainly and bluntly as Jeremiah without drawing upon himself the wrath of his hearers. In defending
himself against his adversaries Jeremiah frequently had recourse
to prayer (for example, 18:19-23; 20:7-12). Among his "confessions" none is franker than the prayer in verses 14-18. Here
the prophet is oppressed because his enemies have been taunting
him. However unfairly these foes treated him, the prophet was
convinced that he himself had been fair to them. He had not
pressed home any claims of his own against them. He had not
petitioned the Almighty to send evil upon them, nor had he
desired "the day of disaster" as though he were merely a calam-
ity-monger. But the word of the Lord had come to him and he
had spoken it faithfully (vs. 16). Actually these were not enemies of Jeremiah but adversaries of God. Therefore the prophet
could rightfully plead: "Let me not be put to shame; let them
be dismayed."

The position of the Sabbath proclamation in verses 19-27,
unrelated to any of the utterances in chapter 17, is illuminated
by the episodes which follow in chapters 18 and 19, each of
which partakes of the nature of a symbolic situation. And this
may account for the fact that this proclamation is included in
the Book of Jeremiah at all, since it probably came from prophetic materials which gathered about Jeremiah, rather than
directly from the prophet himself. Here the action is said to
take place in the Benjamin Gate. The episodes which follow are
described as occurring at the Potter's House (18:1-11), at the
Potsherd Gate near the Valley of Ben-hinnom (19:1-13), and

finally at the upper Benjamin Gate of the house of the Lord (20:1-18).

The prophet is commanded here (17:19-27) to proclaim a message urging the inhabitants of Jerusalem, and the people of the land, as well as their kings, to hallow the Sabbath by refraining from work, and in particular by abstaining from carrying burdens (see Deut. 5:12-14). The royal house and people alike were warned to remember that the welfare and stability of the nation were dependent upon the hallowing of the Sabbath. Their fathers are said to have resisted this divine commandment by refusing to listen. They "stiffened their neck, that they might not hear and receive instruction" (17:23). This generation is warned to avoid their example (vs. 27).

Jeremiah at the Potter's House (18:1-12)

A second episode in this series of symbolic situations describes what Jeremiah learned at the potter's house. The language used to describe this event is particularly instructive. At the time of Jeremiah's call the voice of God was heard speaking to him as a divine Potter to a newly formed vessel (1:5). This idea is now repeated here; for as the potter is working at his wheel ("devising a plan," vs. 11), what "seemed good to the potter to do" (vs. 4) is clearly revealed. The terms "pluck up and break down" (vs. 7) and "build and plant" (vs. 9) are also reminiscent of the divine Potter's words to Jeremiah at the time of his call (1:10). What was said to be true for Jeremiah as an individual is here affirmed to be true for the house of Israel (vs. 6), and is expanded to include any nation or kingdom (vss. 7, 8, 9). The whole scene as here described aptly represents the creative process by the use of three commonplace figures from the workaday world: a potter, the wheel, and clay. The potter is presented as a purposeful worker. The turning wheel is the movement of changing circumstances. The clay can be "spoiled" and "reworked" (vs. 4) as it resists or responds to the hand of the potter. This, in fact, is the most telling point of the portrayal, for the relation between the divine Potter and man can be even more intimate than that between a potter and the clay. A man, or a nation, can give a living response by "turning" with mind and heart to the Creator, amending both ways and doings. This fertile idea of Jeremiah's laid hold on the mind of the Prophet of the Exile (Isa. 45:9; 64:8), and on Paul (Rom. 9:19-24), each of whom developed the idea in his own way.

These main features of Jeremiah 18:1-12 are emphasized by the successive parts of the treatment: The potter at work with the clay provided the prophet with an object lesson of God at work with men. The prophet observed that when a vessel was spoiled the potter would rework the clay into another vessel which met with his approval. Just so, the prophet came to understand, the house of Israel was as clay in the hand of the divine Potter. He saw that God dealt with his people in direct relation to their true character. His intentions for them could be reshaped if they were willing to conform to his will. Thus, God's judgments could be averted when the people turned from evil, just as his promises of good would be withdrawn when they refused to hearken to his commandments. The use of the word "repent" here (vs. 8) deserves special attention. In Jeremiah, God is said to "repent," while men are said to "return"! The Hebrew root for the word "repent" means literally "to be sorry," "to suffer grief," and hence "to repent." Here, as in other instances (for example, Gen. 6:6-7; Jer. 26:3, 13, 19), the term suggests the attitude of God which prompts him to adjust his course of action in dealing with his people. The application of this general principle is made vivid and real in verses 7-10. It was God's intention to judge his people for their sins; therefore they were urged to turn from their evil ways and do good. The obverse of this principle is also true. If God's intention is to build up and plant a people, he is free to change his course of action in dealing with them whenever they fail to heed his ways.

According to 18:12, Jeremiah's proclamation of God's good intentions for his people met a negative response, as the people reaffirmed their determination not to change.

The Plot Devised Against Jeremiah (18:13-23)

Once again in the Book of Jeremiah we find ourselves with two sections of poetry (18:13-17 and 19-23) connected by a prose narrative (18:18).

The Occasion of the Plot: Jeremiah's Protest (18:13-17)

Like Jesus, Jeremiah was a sharp observer of nature. Each of them knew how to draw shrewd and convincing analogies between the world of nature and the character of men. Here Jeremiah draws a sharp contrast between the fidelity of nature and the infidelity of his own people. He likens Israel to a virgin who has done a horrible thing (see 14:17; 31:4, 21) by burning incense unto vanity. (The word for "false gods" in verse 15 really means "non-entities" or "vanity.") He protests that Judah had forgotten the Lord entirely, as shown by the burning of incense to these impotent deities.

The Hebrew text of 18:14-15, as the margin of the Revised Standard Version suggests, is obscure. Jeremiah asks two searching questions: Do the snows of Lebanon fail? Do the mountain waters run dry? Perplexed by the meaning of the Hebrew text, the Greek translator, like so many modern interpreters, used his imagination and arrived at an interesting rendering. He employed the word "breasts" for the Hebrew word rendered "mountain waters" in 18:14: "The breasts of the rock do not give out, do they?" According to the Greek translator, Jeremiah was thinking of the Lebanon and Anti-Lebanon ranges as two unfailing breasts on the bosom of Mother Nature. Their perennial waters perpetually make an oasis of all the adjacent desert wastes. In any case Jeremiah's essential meaning is clear. The constancy of nature is contrasted with the inconstancy of the Covenant people. They had forgotten the unfailing source of their blessings. They had stumbled along bypaths of their own making. They had ignored the highway of their God. They had burned incense to nonentities. Therefore the doom of this generation was already sealed. Their land would become a waste, a thing to be hissed at. As men flee before the east wind from the desert (the Sirocco), so these people would flee before their implacable foes. This calamity would be like seeing God's back in judgment rather than his face in benediction.

The Plot (18:18)

The reply of the people to Jeremiah's message concerning the divine Potter, "We will follow our own plans" (18:12), was reasserted in another way by the leaders in Jerusalem, either in direct response to Jeremiah's predictions of calamity (18:13-17) or as a climax to still other dire threats held over them. To these men the prophet from Anathoth appeared to be an interloper. After all, was it not the business of the priests to expound the Law? Was it not the function of the wise to give counsel? Should not their own prophets interpret the situation as seemed right to them? To resist this meddler in matters which belonged peculiarly to them, they could disregard his words; they would "smite him with the tongue" (circulate slanders about him). The Greek text here omits the word "not" and thus reads: "And carefully watch his words." In this case the meaning would be, "Let us watch for some way in which we may trip him up."

Jeremiah's Reaction to the Plot (18:19-23)

This is the situation which introduces the vindictive lines of 18:19-23. Convinced that the leaders were determined to slay him, the prophet, as on other occasions, voiced his worst fears, as well as the bitterness of his soul, to the One whose call had led him deeper and deeper into conflict with his own people. Actually, Jeremiah felt the attitude of the leaders to be very unreasonable in view of the fact that he had stood as an intercessor for them before God (vs. 20). In the presence of mounting doom he had sought to warn them of their peril. Yet now they had dug a pit for his life. The words which follow are certainly the most bitter imprecation of Jeremiah on record. (For parallels, see some of the "imprecatory Psalms," such as 69, 109, 137.) Is the vindictive character of what he said to be attributed to the gravity of his situation? Or did these maledictions escape from him without restraint in a moment of weakness when his lower nature took command? Or was it that, because he had associated his life so intimately with God's cause, Jeremiah considered his enemies to be God's enemies and so consigned them readily to a dire fate? Whether Jeremiah used words unworthy of his appointment to represent God, or whether he spoke in terms consistent with his vocation, his speech reveals him to be deeply human, a man of passions like unto ourselves.

Jeremiah Breaks the Potter's Flask (19:1-15)

At the potter's house Jeremiah had learned that at one stage on the wheel a spoiled vessel might be reshaped by the potter's hand. Apparently he now recognized that in the hastening events of his day this plastic stage had been passed. Judah, so to speak, was finished, a spoiled vessel, good for nothing but to be broken.

After the manner of the previously recorded symbolic acts, it was by virtue of the word of the Lord that the prophet was told to buy a potter's earthen flask. Delicately constructed with narrow necks, such vessels, once broken, could not be used again. Thus the lesson Jeremiah was to give to the nation had a double meaning. Judah was precious to her Maker but her obduracy had hardened her beyond repair. The vessel was to be broken so that it could never be mended (19:11).

This symbolic act is made all the more impressive by the selection of those who were to witness it as well as by the scene designated for the action. Jeremiah was to take with him elders of the people and some of the senior priests as responsible witnesses. He was to proceed with them to the Potsherd Gate (a place where refuse was dumped) in the Valley of Ben-hinnom. Here he was to break the flask in the sight of the witnesses while he reinforced his act with the tingling words: "Thus says the LORD of hosts: So will I break this people and this city" (19:11).

As for his further instructions, the words of 19:3-9 recall other characteristic utterances of the prophet. One timely expression of judgment follows another. The Hebrew word translated "make void" (vs. 7) is a play on the Hebrew word for "flask." It suggests that the prophet was to empty out the contents of the flask as he spoke and before he broke it. On another occasion Jeremiah had spoken about the high place called Topheth (7:31-32). Josiah in his reforms had defiled Topheth (II Kings 23:10). Now, according to the word to be spoken to the city, it was Jerusalem's turn to be defiled. The houses of Jerusalem and the houses of the kings of Judah, where unclean sacrifices had been offered to other gods, were to be defiled as Topheth had been.

When he had broken the potter's earthen flask and had pronounced his accompanying sentence of doom, Jeremiah proceeded to the court of the Lord's house, and there he repeated his pronouncement.

Jeremiah's Day and Night in the Stocks (20:1-18)

Beginning at 17:19 the reader has been introduced to a sequence of mounting interest in the form of symbolic actions. On the one hand, the actions of the prophet are seen to symbolize the fateful hardening of Judah's heart unto implacable doom. On the other hand, the accompanying "confessions" serve to reveal the tensions and inner conflicts of Jeremiah which came as a direct consequence of fulfilling his vocation as a prophet.

Pashhur Puts Jeremiah in the Stocks (20:1-6)

The signal for open persecution of Jeremiah was given when he was placed in the stocks. Pashhur the priest, who was overseer of the Temple, arrested Jeremiah when he heard his proclamation in the Temple court (19:14-15). Pashhur did his work thoroughly. He regarded Jeremiah as a disturber of the peace within the sacred precincts, possibly also as a threat against the city. He beat Jeremiah and placed him, for punishment, in the stocks at the northern gate of the upper (inner) Temple. This Temple gate is not the same as the city gate of the same name. Here, while it was day, Jeremiah was exposed to the public gaze and to the humiliation, taunts, and insults of the onlookers. Then he was left in the stocks over the following night. These hours of physical pain were not made any easier by his accompanying mental and spiritual distress. The narrative of 20:1-6 provides a context altogether appropriate for a consideration of his "confessions" as they are detailed in the soliloquies of 20:7-18.

The narrative of 20:1-6 centers in what Jeremiah said to Pashhur on the morrow after his night in the stocks. The name Pashhur seems to have been a common one (21:1; 38:1; see Ezra 2:38; Neh. 7:41; 11:12). The name itself (probably of Egyptian origin) means "portion of Horus." When Pashhur came to release the prophet from his aching confinement in the stocks, Jeremiah told him that the Lord was now giving him a new name. Henceforth Pashhur was to be a marked man. Wherever he went he would be known as "Terror on every side." Coming events would give startling confirmation to the Lord's pronouncement from the lips of his prophet. The king of Babylon would execute a judgment upon the Holy City. He would take its treasures as spoil and its people, including Pashhur himself and all his household, as captives. Pashhur would see his friends perish by the sword. By the words "to whom you have prophesied falsely" (20:6), Jeremiah probably referred to strong denials on the part of Pashhur that what Jeremiah had predicted (19:14-15) would come to pass.

The mention of the king of Babylon at this point (20:4) probably indicates that by this time the battle of Carchemish had been fought (see ch. 46 and comments). The ascendancy of Babylon as the overlord of the whole Near Eastern world was now an accomplished fact.

Jeremiah Bewails His Trials (20:7-18)

Among the "confessions" of Jeremiah none reaches more deeply into his personal consciousness, and certainly none discloses more frankly or fully the reality of his communion with God, than his soliloquy recorded in 20:7-18. Are these words to be considered as autobiographic, a faithful record of Jeremiah's mental and spiritual anguish during the night he was confined in the stocks? Or do they rather reflect passing moods to which Jeremiah was subject at various periods of his public career? It is felt by some that the staccato words and abruptly changing moods of the speaker are too extreme to have been uttered on any one occasion. But can anyone be sure of this who has not endured the physical torment of a whole day and night in the stocks, added to the anguish occasioned by the taunts of passersby? Such violently opposed emotions as those expressed in the contrasts of his commitment (vs. 12), singing (vs. 13), and cursing (vs. 14) are not too surprising after all.

Jeremiah's soliloquy begins by a complaint similar to one uttered on another occasion when he asked, "Wilt thou be to me like a deceitful brook?" (15:18). The prophet felt that he had been enticed. At the time of his original encounter with God he had hesitantly responded, yet God was the stronger and had overcome him (1:4-19). Jeremiah indeed had yielded to God's call, yet now he had become a butt of ridicule. Is "laughing-stock" reminiscent of the long hours of the day when Jeremiah had been exposed to the gaze of his mocking countrymen in the Temple court? If he was still in the stocks as he uttered these words, it is likely that he was smarting under the lash of his hostile taunters. The word of the Lord had indeed become a reproach and had made him an object of derision.

Jeremiah now complained that if he spoke the divine word which he had been called to deliver, he was mocked. If he remained silent, then he was burned up within. His statement recorded in 20:9 exhibits a significant characteristic of Hebrew prophecy because it indicates that a prophet could not suppress a message from God (see Amos 3:8). Jeremiah's familiar friends appear to have joined his mockers (20:10). Were they waiting to pounce upon any slip of speech Jeremiah might make, which they might report to the proper authorities and thus be revenged on him "legally"? When his thoughts turned from his persecutors to God, Jeremiah was led to conceive of God as a "dread warrior" who was on his side. True to his word, the Lord would come to the aid of his persecuted spokesman. This seemed to give Jeremiah confidence that his enemies would not be successful in overcoming him. They, and not he, would be shamed when the showdown really came. The Lord, who takes account of a man's affections and thoughts (see 17:9-10), would surely give these tormentors their recompense because Jeremiah was wholly committed to God's cause.

Jeremiah's burst of praise (20:13) in this context need not seem so strange after all, if his thought of his commitment to God as his divine Defender be kept in view. At the time of his call Jeremiah was promised that his enemies would not prevail against him, for God would be with him to deliver him. Did these words of thankful praise now rise in Jeremiah's consciousness as he remembered this? But even praise did not mitigate or change the gravity of his situation. In his desperate plight the prophet winced and cried aloud. Might this violent change of mood have been induced by his cramped physical condition in the stocks? In such a high-strung, sensitive nature as Jeremiah's, tense and violent alternations of feeling, from praising to cursing, would not be unnatural. Like Job, Jeremiah cursed the day on which he was born (see Job 3:1-10). In Jeremiah's case the curse was directed toward the person who announced his birth to his father.

Among the faithful souls who have been persecuted for righteousness' sake, Jeremiah and Job stand out as notable examples. Each, when compelled to plumb the meaning of his own existence, ended with the question, "Why?" And each in his own way fell far short of the example of him who in the final stress said, "Father, forgive them; for they know not what they do" (Luke 23:34).

NARRATIVES AND PRONOUNCEMENTS
(Biographic)
Jeremiah 21:1—29:32
Main Topic: Jeremiah and the Kings, Prophets, and Priests

It is clear that a new section of the book begins here. Furthermore, it is obvious that again topical emphasis rather than any chronological sequence is the organizing feature of the material. The relations between Jeremiah and the various kings of Judah and other civic and religious leaders constitute the dominant center of interest (see Introduction).

At the Beginning of the Siege (21:1-10)

The content of 21:1-10 marks a sudden transition from the undated materials of chapters 14-20 to a specific situation related to the reign of Zedekiah. This narrative describes an event which must have occurred just as the siege of Jerusalem was beginning. These three paragraphs should be read in connection with chapters 34, 37, and 38, which are also dated during the siege of Jerusalem. This passage (21:1-10) probably was placed here, without any direct chronological relation to the preceding materials, when the book was taking shape into its present form, because of the name Pashhur in 21:1 (compare 20:1-6). This Pashhur, however, is identified as the son of Malchiah, whereas the Pashhur of chapter 20 is the son of Immer. The two men do not appear to be at all related.

The situation presents Jeremiah in a role considerably different from that of the harried and persecuted prophet, at midcareer, as portrayed in chapters 14-20. Here, nearing the peak of his career, he has all the stature of an elder statesman whose advice and intercession as a man of God were earnestly sought after by King Zedekiah. Jerusalem now was under siege (or possibly was just about to be besieged) by the Chaldeans (II Kings 25:1-2). Zedekiah, vainly hoping to escape the clutches of Nebuchadnezzar, had sent two members of the royal court to urge Jeremiah to seek divine favor. When Jerusalem had been besieged by Sennacherib the Assyrian, more than a century before this event (701 B.C.), Hezekiah had sent a similar embassy to Isaiah. On that occasion the embassy had met with entirely favorable results (II Kings 19:1-7; Isa. 37:1-7). Was Zedekiah wistfully hoping now for a similar deliverance? Jeremiah could offer no hope to a double-minded king who had failed to heed urgent warnings while there was still time (compare 27:12-15). The prophet therefore declared that, instead, God would support the besieger, smite the city, and deliver Zedekiah and the survivors to the enemy. Furthermore, Jeremiah held out to the people two courses of action: the way of life and the way of death. To desert to the enemy meant life; to resist meant death because the doom of the city was certain.

By advocating submission to Babylon, Jeremiah was by no means a traitor, as succeeding events amply demonstrated. He was consistently maintaining a policy he had advocated ever since Zedekiah had ascended to the throne of David by appointment of Nebuchadnezzar. This was a policy which issued from burning moral convictions. From the beginning (27:1-15) Jeremiah had reminded the king and the representatives of surrounding nations of their obligations to the king of Babylon. Now he was reaffirming the same policy. To Jeremiah, as to all the prophets, an oath made to men (even under stress) was equivalent to an oath to God (compare Jer. 27:1-15 with Ezek. 17:11-21; II Kings 24:17; and II Chron. 36:11-14). Zedekiah had sworn fealty to Nebuchadnezzar, yet he had connived secretly with the Pharaoh of Egypt against the Chaldean king. The consequence is put by Jeremiah in blunt terms: "Thus says the LORD . . . I myself will fight against you . . ." (21:4-5).

Jeremiah and the Dynasty of David (21:11—23:8)

Beginning at 21:11 and continuing through 23:8, Jeremiah's messages to the successive kings of his day are brought together. Just when and where each of these utterances was originally delivered cannot be precisely determined, although each would appear to be contemporaneous with some situation in the life of the king to whom it is addressed. The passage as a whole is very instructive, showing how otherwise occasional and isolated prophecies came to be arranged in their present order because of their topical similarity. The underlying unity of these utterances is indicated by four common features. The first is their dominant appeal. The kings of Judah are urged to "execute justice and righteousness" and thus display the cardinal virtue which was always to distinguish the house of David (compare 21:12; 22:3, 13, 15; 23:5 with Ps. 72:2; Isa. 9:7; 32:1). The second feature these utterances have in common is their basic ethic. The Covenant privileges (for example, permanence and prosperity) are linked to their corresponding Covenant responsibilities (22:3-4; 22:15-16; 22:21; 22:30; 23:5). The third emphasis is their climactic structure. The utterances are strikingly arranged. The whole dynasty of David is addressed first (21:11—

22:9). Then messages delivered to the successive kings of this period are presented in their correct chronological order: Shallum (Jehoahaz, 22:10-12), Jehoiakim (22:13-19), and Coniah (Jehoiachin, 22:24-30). Finally, the kings are addressed as faithless shepherds (23:1-8). Actually Zedekiah is meant. His name is implied indirectly, but in a very significant way. This is indicated by the fourth feature: the Messianic significance of the last utterance. By making a play on the name Zedekiah, one of Jeremiah's most lofty visions of the future of the Covenant people is introduced. The prophet affirms that when the right King comes he will really display the true character of the dynasty of David. His name will be called "The LORD is our righteousness." The Hebrew word for "righteousness" here is strikingly appropriate because of its similarity to the name Zedekiah. Considering the seriousness of the situation which confronted Zedekiah, the last of these kings, the successive messages would be both a warning and a challenge to him. The new king had an opportunity before him, rich in possibilities, if only he would fulfill the meaning of his name.

Jeremiah Addresses the Dynasty of David (21:11—22:9)

Jeremiah begins by addressing the king as a representative of the whole dynasty of David. (Isaiah had addressed Ahaz in a similar fashion; see Isaiah 7:2, 13.) To "execute justice" and "do . . . righteousness" were the ethical foundations of the Davidic kingdom (21:12; 22:3). By urging the whole royal court to do its duty, Jeremiah was pointing out the only sure course toward national security. The expressions "inhabitant of the valley" and "rock of the plain" (21:13) sound strange, but they undoubtedly apply to Jerusalem. Jeremiah's answer to the question, "Who shall come down against us, or who shall enter our habitations?" (21:13), indicates that he was convinced that God would rebuke those who, disregarding their responsibility to him, felt secure.

In the words of 22:1-9, Jeremiah reiterates what he had been saying: justice and righteousness are the foundation of the Davidic throne. By solemn oath (22:5) God had decreed the overthrow of the throne and of the nation unless these words were heeded. He had decreed a destruction as ruinous as if men cut down and burned the forests of Gilead and Lebanon. The desolation would reveal to the nations how faithless the Covenant people had been to their God.

Jeremiah Deplores the Exile of Jehoahaz (22:10-12)

Upon the death of Josiah, the people had proclaimed his third eldest son, Shallum (Jehoahaz), king. But the victorious Pharaoh Neco had deposed and exiled him (II Kings 23:28-33). Jeremiah deplored the captivity of this young king, a captivity from which he would never return. Jehoahaz had reigned only three short months. Jeremiah lamented his fate with even more sorrow than he had shown for the death of his righteous father. There was a finality about the judgment upon Jehoahaz which spoke for itself.

Jeremiah Reproaches Jehoiakim (22:13-19)

Next in order, a stern and courageous message addressed to Jehoiakim is recorded. He had been placed upon the throne by the same Pharaoh Neco who had deposed his younger brother Jehoahaz. According to II Kings 23:33-35, the Pharaoh imposed a tribute of a hundred talents of silver and a talent of gold upon the land. This placed a frightful burden of taxation on the kingdom. Under delusions of grandeur Jehoiakim exacted the silver and the gold from the people of the land while at the same time he was building himself a palace paneled with cedar and painted with vermilion. Jeremiah asked him: "Do you think you are a king because you compete in cedar?" (22:15). Brutal, greedy, and opulent, Jehoiakim was the exact opposite of his father Josiah. His eyes were set on "dishonest gain." His heart was fixed on "shedding innocent blood." He was a gross denial of the noble Davidic ideal of justice and righteousness. Therefore he was doomed to an untimely and disgraceful end.

It is not clear to whom the words of 22:20-23 are addressed, but they affirm the same principle for which Jeremiah has been pleading. The kings are rebuked for refusing to hearken to the voice of their divine Benefactor. The fate of these rulers (shepherds) would confound them. Although Judah felt secure, like a bird nested high in the cedars of Lebanon, such self-confidence would shortly be turned into anguish. The Hebrew word translated "prosperity" in 22:21 really means "security," "rest," or "ease." God's word spoken to Judah in her prosperous days had not been heeded. Now a sore judgment had already come upon her.

Jeremiah Warns Jehoiachin (22:24-30)

Jehoiachin (Coniah) had succeeded his father as king of Judah. He and his mother, the widow of Jehoiakim, were the unhappy victims of Jehoiakim's folly. The sober words addressed to the young king, only eighteen years old, were fulfilled when he and the queen mother were taken captive by the Chaldeans in 597 B.C. (II Kings 24:8-16). Yet, as reigning king, Jehoiachin was the responsible incumbent of the Davidic throne. Jeremiah declared that though he were like a signet ring upon the right hand of God, even so he would be torn off and given over to judgment at the hands of the Chaldeans. Like a broken pot or a useless vessel, Jehoiachin would be hurled away. There was, moreover, a certain finality about Jehoiachin's personal calamity. Although actually he was not childless, dynastically he was. He would provide no successor to the Davidic throne. Therefore his obituary might just as well be written now in the annals of the land.

Jeremiah, Zedekiah, and the Ideal Ruler (23:1-8)

Zedekiah, who succeeded Jehoiachin by appointment of Nebuchadnezzar, was a younger son of Josiah, while Jehoiachin was Josiah's grandson. From the perspective of the whole basic passage (21:11—23:8), what Jeremiah means by "shepherds" here is clear. He had mentioned successively all the kings of Judah during his prophetic career: Josiah, Jehoahaz, Jehoiakim, Jehoiachin. Without mentioning Zedekiah by name, Jeremiah now rebuked these rulers who, like unworthy shepherds, had failed to feed the flock of God and instead had scattered them. Because they were primarily responsible for Judah's present woes, these faithless leaders would be superseded. God himself would gather and provide for his scattered flock. He would raise up the true offspring of David—the Messiah, a righteous Branch. This word "Branch" literally means "that which grows." It may also be translated "Sprout" or "Shoot." The term, as used also by Isaiah (4:2; compare Jer. 33:15), lends a creative touch to any situation in which it figures. Judah was facing a prospect bleak and arid indeed. But the prophet was sustained by an unshakable confidence in the righteousness of God. In due time the dried-up twig of David's dynasty would put forth a "Shoot." That which grows inherently from God embodies his own characteristics, therefore the "Shoot" would, like the Creator, be righteous. The coming King consequently would embody the actual characteristics of the ideal which had been announced to David and his seed. He would reign wisely, with justice and righteousness. True to his name, "The LORD is our righteousness," he would qualify as the ideal King. A restoration, provided by a new exodus more glorious than the deliverance from Egypt, was thus in store for God's people (see 16:14-15).

Jeremiah Upbraids the False Prophets (23:9-40)

Jeremiah was stirred by the failure of still other leaders of the Covenant people, those who ostensibly were appointed to be spokesmen for the Lord. Within the broader scope of the book these men are referred to frequently as "prophets": 2:8; 5:30-31; 6:13-14; 8:10-11; 14:13-15; 18:18. In chapters 26 and 27 they are mentioned often. In chapter 28, Hananiah, the son of Azzur, a prophet from Gibeon, is branded as false. In chapter 29, Ahab, the son of Kolaiah, and Zedekiah, the son of Maaseiah, are scored for prophesying falsely to the exiles in Babylon. Here (23:9-40) Jeremiah mentions no names, but speaks of these men as a class of professionals.

"Their might is not right" (23:9-15)

Jeremiah felt shattered and overcome by the necessity of declaring God's holy message against the transgressions of certain prophets and priests who profaned the Temple by their godless lives. This ungodly manner of life was due to their infidelity in personal relations ("adultery") and to their unfeigned hypocrisy (they "walk in lies"). These men, so the prophet declared, would be driven by their own sins into "slippery paths in the darkness," and so to their own undoing. Certain prophets from Samaria openly advocated Baal worship, while other prophets, of Jerusalem, were guilty of immorality and deceit. In this way they not only strengthened the hands of evildoers but even confirmed them in their ways. These men would be fed with wormwood, which is to say they would suffer bitter calamity and sorrow, as though they had been given poisoned water to drink.

"I did not send the prophets, yet they ran" (23:16-22)

On other occasions Jeremiah had warned against men in high

place who cried, "Peace, peace," when there was no peace (6:14; 8:11). Now he warned against men who spoke "visions of their own minds, not from the mouth of the LORD," filling the people with false hopes. Such indifference to realities led Jeremiah to denounce these men as imposters. True prophets "stood in the council of the LORD," which means that they received their messages from a source higher than themselves. The message came to them as they perceived and heard the divine word (23:18). Such men gave heed to God's word by embodying it in their own personal experience. Jeremiah protested that some men had not even been sent, "yet they ran." Had they really stood in the "council" of the Lord, they would have proclaimed his word, not their own, to the people, and so would have turned them from their evil way.

"The prophets ... prophesy lies in my name" (23:23-32)

Since God is not subject to human limitations but is present everywhere, Jeremiah proclaimed that no one could escape the divine gaze. Therefore God was acquainted with the lying pretensions of these men who, when they said, "I have dreamed," professed to have authentic revelations of God's will. Jeremiah certainly did not mean to discount the dream as one authentic mode of prophetic revelation. On one occasion he himself professed to have received the divine word in this way (31:26). But he did denounce the practice in which these men indulged—the practice of claiming to have a higher source for their messages when they really had none at all. By this duplicity they had emptied a true vehicle of divine communication of its significance (Num. 12:6). They caused God's people to forget his revealed character (name) just as Baal worship had corrupted their fathers' understanding of him. Therefore Jeremiah insisted that the dream and the word of God must be sharply distinguished, as straw is distinguished from wheat. An authentic revelation is known by its effects. A fire consumes whatever it touches. A hammer-blow upon a rock breaks it in pieces. So, too, God's word is known by what it does. When men give secondhand messages as their own, or tell lying dreams as though they were God's truth, let them know that the Lord is against them.

"You are the burden" (23:33-40)

The Hebrew word for "burden" means "load," "lifting," or

"bearing." The word, as used in a technical sense in prophecy, suggests the idea of catastrophe, destruction, or the judgment of God, and has an ominous import (see, for example, Isa. 13:1; 15:1; 17:1). The burden came from God to the prophet, but it did not remain with him; he in turn raised it or lifted it or laid it upon an individual or nation. Here Jeremiah forbade the people to use the word "burden" for an utterance lest they profane it. By current practice, evidently, men were accustomed to greet a prophet by saying, "What is the burden of the LORD?" This practice had now become so perverted, so emptied of its true connotation, that Jeremiah used the phrase to rebuke its users. When they asked, "What is the burden of the LORD?", Jeremiah was to reply, "You are the burden," and add God's further word: "I will cast you off" (23:33).

Jeremiah Sees Two Baskets of Figs (24:1-10)

Some of Jeremiah's most significant messages are connected with things which he saw—whether commonplace, like the stork in the heavens, the potter's vessel, the plowman's yoke; or singular, like the "early-awake" tree, the boiling cauldron, the baskets of figs. In this case the vision is of two baskets of figs placed before the Temple of the Lord. The figs were of two kinds: very good, like first-ripe figs; and very bad, so bad they could not be eaten. As for their position, they were placed before the Temple of the Lord. All these aspects taken together are necessary for a true understanding of this experience. That it was not merely a subjective vision is suggested by two concurrent expressions: The affirmation of verse 1: "The LORD showed me"; and the question of verse 3: "What do you see, Jeremiah?"

The position of the figs before the Temple of the Lord suggests that their value is to be found in the fact that they were to be offered to God. As symbols of two classes of people, the exiles in Babylon and the remnant in Jerusalem are subordinate to the focal point. What really made the difference between the two classes of people was their "heart." The good figs were those who would return to the Lord with their whole heart (24:7). In his letter to the exiles, written apparently about this same time (compare 24:1 and 29:1-2), the prophet said: "For thus says the LORD . . . You will seek me and find me; when you seek me with all your heart" (29:10, 13). Jeremiah's hope is seen to be grounded in genuine ethical convictions. He knew that God was not going to work any magic. He knew, too, that the people who were fortunate enough to have escaped exile did not enjoy this privilege because of any goodness on their part, as though they were "good figs." Nor were the exiles suffering just because they were "bad figs." He saw that God's providential and disciplinary actions upon his people in the end would do their own work. He was confident that *there would be a real return to God on the part of some people;* and when this perceptible change took place, in actual ethical fulfillment of Covenant relations, then there could also be a return to the land where the Covenant people could be built up and firmly planted (1:10). The prophet was convinced that under the chastening disciplines of exile, a real and effective change in the essential relation of the Covenant people to God could and would take place. Therefore they were like the basket of good figs before the Temple of the Lord. The miserable remnant of the people who had been left in the land were like bad figs, so bad they could not be eaten. It merely remained for them to be cast out, to become "a reproach, a byword, a taunt, and a curse in all the places" where they should be driven (24:9-10). Jeremiah's vision of the two baskets of figs, so simple, so commonplace, and so unadorned, reveals his grasp of the genuine prophetic faith. Communion with God and the blessings of his unfailing grace are independent of institutions, forms, and places like the Temple with its sacrifices, or even the Promised Land. Whenever God is sought with the whole heart, though it be in exile, there he may be found (see Deut. 4:20-31; 6:4-5; Ps. 119:2, 10).

Jeremiah at Mid-Career (25:1-38)

The battle of Carchemish was a decisive turning point in the history of the whole Near Eastern world. After the fall of Nineveh in 612 B.C., the Assyrian Empire was destroyed, never to rise again. Egypt then made a new bid for world empire; Pharaoh Neco's mercenary legions marched northward. King Josiah of Judah, attempting to stop him at Megiddo, perished (609 B.C.). This was the fourth year of King Jehoiakim of Judah. It was also the first year of Nebuchadnezzar as king of Babylon. His father, Nabopolassar, had died soon after the battle of Carchemish.

At this moment, so significant for his own nation as well as

for all the peoples of the Near Eastern world, Jeremiah, who at
the time of his call had been "appointed . . . a prophet to the
nations" (1:5, 10), once again received the word of the Lord.
Chapter 25 is important because it offers a summary of Jeremiah's proclamations for the first twenty-three years of his public
ministry. It also points ominously forward to the role of Babylon
as the political and military overlord of the entire Near East.

Whether any part of this chapter was included in the first
scroll, written in 604 B.C. and destroyed by Jehoiakim, cannot
be determined (36:1-8). It is difficult, also, to say how much of
this chapter was included in the second scroll Jeremiah dictated
to Baruch in the fifth year of Jehoiakim while they were in hiding
(36:1, 9, 27-32; compare 36:29-30 with 25:8-14). What Jeremiah set down in writing at that time was probably revised after
the fall of Jerusalem. In this way the content of chapter 25 took
shape in its present form.

That this is a serious problem in the study of this book is
indicated by the striking difference at this point between the
present Hebrew text and the Greek text (Septuagint Version) of
Jeremiah. After the words "in this book" (25:13a), the Greek
text includes chapters 46:1—51:64. The prophecies concerning
the nations are introduced in the Greek text in the following
order: Elam, 49:34-39; Egypt, 46:2-28; Babylon, 50-51; Philistia, 47:1-7; Edom, 49:7-22; Ammon, 49:1-6; Kedar, 49:28-33;
Damascus, 49:23-27; Moab, 48:1-47. Historical study of the
text has established the fact that these prophecies concerning the
nations (chs. 46-51) stood at one time in the Hebrew text (as they
also do in the Septuagint Version) immediately following the
words "everything written in this book" (25:13). In the Greek
text the collection of messages concerning the nations is introduced by a heading: "That which Jeremiah prophesied against
all the nations." When these prophecies were removed by Hebrew editors of the text to the end of the book, this heading
apparently was left in its present position in the Hebrew text
instead of being lifted along with the prophecies to which it belongs. Hence chapter 25:1-13, which originally concluded a book
about Jeremiah's prophecies concerning "all the people of Judah"
(25:1, 9), now stands in the Hebrew and English texts as an
introduction to messages concerning the surrounding nations.

The content of this chapter, as the reader of the English Bible
now finds it, may be divided as follows:

1. Jeremiah's messages for twenty-three years to all the people of Judah are summarized (vss. 1-7).
2. Nebuchadnezzar is proclaimed as the overlord for seventy years of the whole Near Eastern world (vss. 8-12).
3. A transition, in three parts:
   a. The original conclusion of verses 1-12 (vs. 13a).
   b. The original introduction to the messages to the nations, verses 15-38 (vs. 13b).
   c. An editorial parenthesis (vs. 14).
4. Jerusalem and the surrounding nations symbolically are made to drink from the cup of the Lord's wrath (vss. 15-29).
5. The Lord's indictment against all the nations of the earth is pronounced (vss. 30-38).

The reader of the English text, therefore, finds in Jeremiah chapter 25 a graphic summary of Jeremiah's ministry up to the time of the battle of Carchemish. Here, also, the tone is set for all of Jeremiah's ministry thereafter, by linking the fate of Judah with the destiny of Babylon as God's appointed servant.

Jeremiah's Twenty-Three-Year Ministry to Judah (25:1-7)

The summary of Jeremiah's prophecies (25:1-13) may be considered first. For twenty-three years Jeremiah had been a spokesman for the Lord, urging the Covenant people to turn from false worship. The words "turn" and "dwell" express a characteristic note in Jeremiah's preaching. To the prophet from Anathoth, penitence was the condition of permanence. Persistently the ever-wakeful God had been reiterating to the people of Judah, through his servants the prophets, the conditions they must fulfill if they would enjoy permanently the privileges of the Covenant. Yet the Covenant people, just as persistently, had not listened but instead had lusted after other gods. To worship the works of their own hands was not only to build "cisterns . . . broken cisterns," which could hold no water (2:13), but was also to provoke God to anger. This is strong language, but it is so characteristic of Jeremiah that a summary may well be given.

1. To offer worship to other gods is to provoke the Lord to anger (25:6-7; compare 7:18-19; 8:19; 11:17; 32:29-32; 44:3-8).
2. The Lord's wrath is like a cup of fury which the nations

must drink (25:15-16, 28); it is like a consuming fire (4:4; 21:12); it is like a whirling tempest (23:19; 30:23); it is like fury poured out on the remnant of Judah gone astray (42:18-19).

3. The Lord's anger is fierce (25:37-38), despoiling pastures and devastating peaceful folds. Like a lion searching for prey, like a sword which devours, the Lord's anger is fierce.

The language of 25:1-7, therefore, serves to emphasize the polarities of God's character as proclaimed by Jeremiah during the first half of his prophetic ministry. God is infinitely gracious and patient; he is inexorably just. Because Jeremiah saw his world in the blaze of God's justice, he used clear, blunt words, like "fury" and "fire," to stay his impenitent generation on its mad course of impiety.

Nebuchadnezzar, "My Servant" (25:8-14)

To understand how decisive Jeremiah considered the battle of Carchemish to be, the reader of this book may well connect chapter 46 with 25:1-14, for both passages are dated in the fourth year of Jehoiakim (46:2). There the forces of Egypt are pictured as a river whose surging waters would desire to rise and cover the earth. Instead they are said to have been drawn to the north country at the River Euphrates where the Lord God of Hosts had determined to hold a sacrifice. Thus Egypt was frustrated at Carchemish as by divine decree. Pharaoh, king of Egypt, thenceforth was to be known by the name: "Noisy one who lets the hour go by" (46:17).

According to Jeremiah 25:8-14, Nebuchadnezzar was destined to be more than a victor at Carchemish. Now he had become the appointed agent of the Lord of Hosts and was called by him "my servant." He was to execute judgment upon the Covenant people by laying their land waste, and also the land of the surrounding nations. So completely was he to do his work that all of the familiar signs of civilized life would disappear (25:10). The tenure of his appointment would be seventy years. Then the king of Babylon also would come under judgment of the Lord of all the earth, who would make his land "an everlasting waste."

The Cup of the Wine of God's Wrath (25:15-29)

By using the figure of an intoxicating cup of wrath to describe judgment, the character and scope of the doom hovering over the nations of the Near Eastern world is now described (compare 13:12-14; 49:12; 51:7). Symbolically the cup is pressed upon nation after nation, beginning at Jerusalem. All the nations to whom special messages are addressed in chapters 46-51 are mentioned here except Damascus. Kedar, a tribe (49:28-33), is addressed here for Arabia. In addition, the following nations are included in this symbolic pressing of the cup of wrath to their lips: Uz (closely connected with Edom); Tyre and Sidon; Dedan and Tema (north Arabian tribes); Buz and "all who cut the corners of their hair" (probably desert tribes); Zimri (unknown); Elam and Media (far to the east). In the Hebrew text Babylon is referred to as "Sheshach" (25:26, margin), a cryptic name or cipher. The petty and rapacious schemes of the nations are now said to be their undoing (compare Jer. 46:7-12; 48: 26-33; 49:20-22), and they reel under judgment like drunken men. None can escape from drinking the cup. If any nations should refuse they are to be told: "Thus says the LORD of hosts: You must drink!" (25:28).

The Lord's Controversy with the Nations (25:30-38)

As the mood of the prophet changes from prose to rhythm, so also the figure changes from the cup of wrath to the roaring lion. Like a wild beast who roars as he approaches his prey (vs. 30), like a lion who has left his covert (vs. 38), the Lord is pictured as roaring mightily against his fold. He is also represented as shouting. This time the shout is likened to that of the vintage treaders as they press the grapes. The world-wide claims of the divine sovereignty are pressed home even more impressively as the Lord is represented as a prosecutor reading his indictment against the nations. He declares that judgment is to be pronounced upon entire humanity ("all flesh"). Neither rulers ("shepherds"), nor rich and influential people ("lords of the flock"), will escape the overwhelming doom, for like "choice rams" they shall fall, and their resources ("pasture," "peaceful folds") shall be devastated, as by the stirring of a great tempest.

Jeremiah Preaches in the Temple (26:1-24)

Early in Jehoiakim's reign Jeremiah delivered a passionate sermon in the Temple court. Only three months had passed since

Josiah's untimely death. Jehoahaz had been removed from the throne and sent in chains to Egypt by the victorious Pharaoh Neco. Jehoiakim had been enthroned in his stead. Jeremiah now stepped into full public light as a statesman of intrepid courage and political insight. Chapter 26 dramatizes why and how he was put on trial for his life. Chapter 7 records in greater detail what he said on this momentous occasion.

Jeremiah's Sermon Summarized (26:1-6)

The prophet stood at a gate between the inner and outer courts of the Temple (7:2; compare I Kings 7:12), apparently at the time of an appointed fast. He was inspired to speak boldly, for God was about to act (for "repent," 26:3, see comment on 18:1-6). Jeremiah proclaimed that: (1) God had been urgently warning his people by his servants the prophets. (2) His people had not given heed to his revealed word, whether in law or by prophet. (3) God proposed to destroy the Temple as he had uprooted Shiloh (see comment on 7:14). (4) God would make Jerusalem a curse "for all the nations of the earth."

Jeremiah Is Arrested (26:7-11)

This was probably the first time Jeremiah had predicted openly that God would destroy both Temple and city. It must have sounded in the ears of his hearers much like blasphemy and treason. For them the Temple was inviolate! This popular conviction, persistent since the days of Isaiah, had now become an empty obsession. The city was holy! Was it not destined to become a blessing to the whole earth? Jeremiah had violated the strongest religious and patriotic prejudices of his people. And what will men not do rather than give up their prejudices? Such a twofold calamity was to them unthinkable. At all costs God must protect his house; he must defend their city. Anyone who questioned this must be dealt with. And so the cry went up: "You shall die!" The priests and prophets arrested Jeremiah. But the people had not yet made up their minds: "And all the people gathered about Jeremiah in the house of the LORD" (26:9).

Jeremiah Is Tried and Vindicated (26:12-19)

The princes—officials of the court, and probably counselors to the king (see 36:11-19)—now appeared upon the scene. They took their seat at the New Gate, probably the high or upper gate mentioned also in 20:2 (see II Kings 15:35), where judgment usually was pronounced upon offenders. Jeremiah now had an opportunity to defend himself before the princes, who had been joined by representatives of the people (26:12). When priests and prophets had made the charge that Jeremiah was worthy of the sentence of death for prophesying "against this city," Jeremiah made his reply. The Lord had sent him! If they would amend their ways and doings, then neither of the dire consequences he had predicted would come to pass. Jeremiah must have known, even before he spoke, that he had taken his life in his hands. But he did not hesitate. Like Luther centuries later, and many other courageous souls, Jeremiah stood firmly, like an iron pillar, upon the sure word of God.

Jeremiah's bold defense and intrepid spirit were irresistible, and convinced the princes and people. Moreover, certain "elders of the land" (probably heads of leading families, or venerable persons respected for their wisdom and judgment) now asserted themselves. They cited the convincing example of Micah of Moresheth, who, about a century before this event, had also spoken a severe message in the name of the Lord of hosts. But King Hezekiah and the people had heeded his word, and Jerusalem had been spared. The citation of this historical precedent proved to be decisive. Jeremiah was released and was taken under the protection of Ahikam the son of Shaphan (II Kings 22:12), apparently a man of commanding influence (see 26:24).

The Fate of Uriah (26:20-24)

But what was Jehoiakim's attitude toward the prophet? The time had not yet come for him and Jeremiah to clash. This was to happen later (chapter 36). But to show how perilous Jeremiah's position was, now that he had spoken the word of the Lord so boldly, the case of Jehoiakim's ruthless treatment of Uriah from Kiriath-jearim is cited as an appendix to the Temple Sermon incident. Uriah had spoken "in words like those of Jeremiah." But unfortunately Uriah did not have the courage to stand his ground like the iron pillar of Anathoth. He fled to Egypt, but Jehoiakim had him brought back and slew him.

Verse 24 belongs to the narrative in 26:12-19.

The Final Warnings (27:1—29:32)

The narrative of chapters 27, 28, and 29 is related to events which occurred early in the reign of Zedekiah, soon after the captivity of Jehoiachin and the exile of the ten thousand chief people of the land (II Kings 24:10-17). Nebuchadnezzar had appointed Mattaniah, one of the youngest sons of Josiah, as king of Judah and had changed his name to Zedekiah. The precise timing of the narrative is given in 28:1. The critical nature of this situation is indicated by the fact that Zedekiah had sent an embassy to Nebuchadnezzar in the persons of Elasah, the son of Shaphan, and Gemariah, the son of Hilkiah (29:3). Zedekiah himself had also gone to Babylon in the fourth year of his reign (51:59). Whether he had been summoned to appear or had gone voluntarily is not stated. Meanwhile ferment was seething among the nations of the Fertile Crescent. Envoys from five surrounding nations had come to Jerusalem to Zedekiah either to plan a strategy of resistance or to foment open rebellion (27:1-3).

Two features of Jeremiah's messages are stressed. First, by divine decree the sovereignty of Nebuchadnezzar over the whole Near Eastern world is reaffirmed (see 25:9). Second, this radical proclamation on the part of Jeremiah is resisted by certain unnamed prophets (27:14, 16), and also by Hananiah, the son of Azzur, of Gibeon, who opposed Jeremiah violently (28:1-17). Jeremiah also was opposed in an exchange of letters by certain leaders among the exiles in Babylon.

Jeremiah Warns the Surrounding Nations (27:1-11)

The use of the name Zedekiah instead of Jehoiakim in verse 1 (see margin) is amply justified by the context that follows (27:3, 12, 20; 28:1). Jeremiah was led to use a dramatic device to proclaim God's message to the surrounding nations. Envoys had come to Jerusalem from the kings of Edom, Moab, Ammon, Tyre, and Sidon, ostensibly to form an alliance to resist the king of Babylon. After making wooden yoke-bars with leather thongs, such as are worn by oxen, Jeremiah appeared in public with them (as he also did later in the Temple, 28:1, 10, 12). In this symbolic way he was to send messages to the kings, through their envoys, saying that any conspiracy among them to throw off the yoke of Babylon would be fatal. The yoke-bars and thongs, he declared, represented Nebuchadnezzar's right to rule by divine decree (27:4-7). The king of Babylon was the appointed agent of the one sovereign God, the Lord of Hosts, the God of Israel. In due time this king himself would be judged. But now, to resist him was to rebel against God. Jeremiah classed their prophets with their diviners, dreamers, soothsayers, and sorcerers, showing with what scorn the man from Anathoth regarded men who had not been sent by the Lord with a real message for the people. Such men, according to Jeremiah, were speaking lying words and were not to be heeded. The nations which wore the Babylonian yoke would enjoy security within their own borders by the decree of the same God who had now proclaimed Nebuchadnezzar as his servant (27:8-11).

Jeremiah Addresses Zedekiah (27:12-15)

Jeremiah's use of the first person "I" in 27:12 and 16 makes his message all the more emphatic. When he admonishes Zedekiah, "Bring your necks under the yoke of the king of Babylon," he is probably referring to the attempted conspiracy among the envoys of the surrounding nations. False prophets apparently were putting pressure upon Zedekiah to join in an alliance with these kings. If, as it appears, Zedekiah was seeking to maintain a show of good relations with the king of Babylon, Jeremiah's advice is all the more severe (29:3; 51:59).

Jeremiah Cautions Both Priests and People (27:16-22)

The same false prophets were seeking to build up public opinion among the priests and the people by glowing predictions that before long the Temple treasures would be returned to Jerusalem. In 597 B.C., Jeconiah (Jehoiachin), the nobles of Judah, and many people had been deported to Babylon (II Kings 24:10-17). The Temple also had been despoiled of its treasures. Now, only four years after this catastrophe (28:1), these prophets were predicting to priests and people alike that presently these very vessels would be returned to the Temple. Jeremiah suggested that if such men were true prophets they would intercede now with the Lord of Hosts that no more sacred vessels be removed, because the remaining Temple treasures also were doomed. They would be carried away to Babylon. Worse days were in store for Jerusalem and the Temple. Eventually, it was true, they would be restored, but only when God decreed that they should be restored.

Jeremiah Is Opposed by Hananiah (28:1-32)

The heading of chapter 28, introduced by the words "In that
same year," connects the episode related in this chapter with
the warnings given in chapter 27. Hananiah, the son of Azzur,
an inhabitant of Gibeon, now came forward to rebuke Jeremiah
publicly for the words he had spoken about the vessels of the
Temple. Hananiah, a popular advocate of nationalistic aspirations, contradicted Jeremiah. He declared, in the name of the
Lord of Hosts, the God of Israel, that within two years all the
sacred Temple vessels taken to Babylon by Nebuchadnezzar
would be returned to Jerusalem. With them also would come
Jehoiachin and all the exiles from Judah, for the yoke of the
king of Babylon would be broken (28:1-4).

Jeremiah's hearty "Amen" indicates how sincerely he wished
Hananiah's prediction could come to pass. He, too, loved his own
people and his native land. Nevertheless, the Lord had revealed
to him that his people and his land were to experience severer
judgments. As a true prophet he could not reverse his word.
Either he or Hananiah must be in error. Jeremiah, therefore,
cited the recognized test of a true prophet (Deut. 18:22; compare Deut. 13:1-3). A true prophet's word would come to pass,
whether that word were judgment (vs. 8) or peace (vs. 9).
Hananiah, as though to dramatize his own prediction, and possibly also to break Jeremiah's confidence that he himself spoke
in the name of the Lord, broke the wooden yoke-bars Jeremiah
was wearing. At the same time Hananiah declared that within
two full years God would break the yoke of Nebuchadnezzar
from off the neck of all the nations. Jeremiah having been thus
publicly humiliated went his way. He had no counterword to
speak at the moment (vss. 10-11). But in due time Jeremiah
was prepared to give Hananiah a very startling answer. He confronted Hananiah with the divine word which had been given
to him. By his rash act Hananiah had but symbolized severer
judgments to come. He had broken wooden yoke-bars, but in
their place God had forged bars of iron. God's judgment pronounced against the nations could not be broken. The nations
were destined to serve Nebuchadnezzar as the agent of the Lord
of all creation. And now Jeremiah was ready to make a drastic
prediction about Hananiah himself. The Lord had not sent Hananiah, but he was about to send him. The Lord would remove him

from the face of the earth! He had spoken rebellion against the Lord. Only two months later Hananiah died. "Two years . . . two months . . ." Grim end!

Jeremiah Corresponds with the Exiles (29:1-32)

About the same time that Jeremiah was uttering the warnings recorded in chapters 24 (see comment), 27, and 28, he sent a letter in a similar vein, addressed to all exiles in Babylon (29:1-2). He mentioned specifically the elders, the priests, the prophets, and all the people. He also made a reply to a letter sent by a certain Shemaiah of Nehelam. This exchange of letters is one of the few examples of such correspondence preserved in the Old Testament (compare II Kings 19:14).

This correspondence throws light upon the conditions of the captives in Babylon. No indication is given of why Zedekiah had sent envoys to Babylon at this time (29:3). But Jeremiah took advantage of the occasion to send his communication with them. Elasah was brother of Ahikam, the prince-friend of Jeremiah who protected him after his arrest and trial for preaching the Temple Sermon (26:1-24). Gemariah was the son of Hilkiah. He could hardly have been Jeremiah's brother. He was probably the son of the Hilkiah (the high priest, of the house of Zadok) who had found the Book of the Law (II Kings 22).

In this bold, discerning letter Jeremiah urged the exiles in the name of the Lord of Hosts, the God of Israel, to entertain no false hopes about a speedy return to their homeland. They were to settle down to normal life by building houses and planting gardens and raising families. Furthermore, they were to seek the welfare of the land in which they lived, for its welfare would contribute to their own. They were not to be deceived by false prophets or diviners who proclaimed only empty dreams. Their word was a lying word, for the Lord did not send them.

This letter must have been heard with consternation wherever it was read among the exiles. Their plight was unenviable. According to competent archaeological evidence it is impossible to exaggerate their sufferings. They were settled along broken-down and unused canals which had deteriorated into swamp land, infested with malaria and mosquitoes. The humidity was high, and in summer the heat rose to about one hundred and twenty degrees. But the stark realism of such a physical context makes Jeremiah's letter all the more appealing, for he immediately turns to the real plans which the Lord has for his people and their future.

Did Jeremiah anticipate how these words would likely be received by the exiles? Who can say? At any rate he sounded a note which rings with genuine realism. He reiterated in this letter what he had affirmed in a slightly different way in his parable of the two baskets of figs (ch. 24). God's intentions for his people, Jeremiah declared, were not to be interpreted either by their present circumstances, drastic though they were, nor by the length of the exile (seventy years is doubtless meant to be an approximate number; compare 29:10 with 25:12). Actually God had plans for his people, plans which contemplated their welfare and not their hurt. According to his wise designs the Covenant people were to have both a hope and a future. Therefore, let them call upon God and he will hear them. The reality of his presence, the privilege of communion, the blessings of his grace, were not circumscribed by place or time. Even in this strange land, amid sorrows, frustrations, and physical distress, God could be sought and found when his people would seek him with all their heart.

Once again the common sense and sound spirituality of Jeremiah are to be seen. He steadfastly affirmed that the Covenant God was not capricious, nor was there any cult magic available by which he could be used, coerced, or controlled. Relations with him must begin, and be maintained, on the level of ethical action. God indeed did search the heart. He did take account of men's thoughts and intentions (see 17:9-10 and comments). With the whole heart men were to seek and find God, because the love of God was always seeking to awaken the return-love of man.

The passage recorded in 29:15-19 repeats what Jeremiah had said already to the inhabitants of Jerusalem in his parable of the baskets of figs. The citizens left in Jerusalem, including their king, were like vile figs, so bad they could not be eaten. Their doom was sealed, not by any arbitrary decree of God, but by their own essential character. Nor was this doom the consequence of any single or isolated act. They had not listened to God's words, persistently sent to them by his servants the prophets (see 25:1-7 and comments). Jeremiah also proclaimed a further word of the Lord to the exiles. Two immoral and presumptuous prophets, Ahab the son of Kolaiah, and Zedekiah the son of Maaseiah, were rebuked for prophesying a lie unto the exiles in the name of the Lord. By so doing they had committed folly in Israel and would meet an untimely end, being roasted in fire at the hands of Nebuchadnezzar (29:20-23).

A further example of correspondence between Jeremiah and the exiles is recorded in 29:24-32. It refers to one immediate reaction to Jeremiah's words in his letter concerning the length of the siege and his advice to "build houses and live in them, and plant gardens and eat their produce" (29:28). A certain Shemaiah, an exile from Nehelam, was incensed by these words, and wrote to Zephaniah, the priest in Jerusalem who was now chief officer of the Temple. He complained that Jeremiah was like an irresponsible madman who should be clapped into the stocks and collar. He commanded Zephaniah to rebuke Jeremiah and take appropriate action. It is said that Zephaniah, who apparently was a friend of the prophet, or who at least regarded his advice to the exiles as sound, read the letter to Jeremiah but did nothing more. However, Jeremiah replied personally to the exiles, asking that they give no heed to Shemaiah's words or actions. Shemaiah had not been sent by the Lord. He would lead them to trust in a lie. Because he had "talked rebellion against the LORD," neither he nor any of his descendants would live to see the good which the Lord proposed to do to his people. Thus the fate of Shemaiah of Nehelem would be as severe in the end as that which, for a similar reason, overtook Hananiah.

PROPHETIC UTTERANCES AND NARRATIVES
(Biographic)
Jeremiah 30:1—40:6
Main Topic: The Siege and Fall of Jerusalem

As in other sections of this book, topical emphasis is the main organizing feature here. No attempts seem to have been made in the composition of this section to relate the parts in any temporal sequence, for they are quite disjointed chronologically (see Introduction).

The Book of Consolation (30:1—33:26)

Chapters 30-33 present the most hopeful utterances among Jeremiah's prophecies. In fact, they are well termed a "book of consolation," where Jeremiah's prophetic inspiration rises to its most lofty expression. The events described in chapters 32 and 33, with their associated prophecies, are precisely dated (32:1; 33:1) within the siege of Jerusalem and should be read in connection with chapters 37 and 38. But chapters 30 and 31 are not dated. They contemplate the future from a point of view probably after the fall of Jerusalem, amid the ashes and ruin of the nation. The manner in which the pains of judgment and the promises of restoration are interwoven to illustrate both the severity and the goodness of God indicates that the content of chapters 32 and 33 is topically arranged.

"Write in a book all the words" (30:1-3)

Upon other occasions Jeremiah, at divine command, had recorded prophecies of judgment (for example, 36:2, 6, 28; see 25:13). Now he was directed to record promises of restoration which included both Israel and Judah. The fortunes of the stricken Covenant people were to be restored when the Covenant God brought them back to the land which he had given to their fathers.

How much of this material stems directly from Jeremiah himself, as the word of the Lord came to him in the early days of the Exile while he contemplated the woes of Judah, and how much is to be considered as revelations of the same God made to his immediate successors later in the Exile, has been keenly debated. Suffice it to say now that the same dominant notes sounded elsewhere in the Book of Jeremiah are resounded here. They are well summed up in the words which first broke forth in the consciousness of Jeremiah at the time of his call (1:10).

These utterances came to be arranged in their present topical order as so many variations on the dual theme—"to pluck up . . . and to plant." Had the children of Israel been just another nation on the earth, it is not too much to say that as a people they would have passed into oblivion at the fall of Jerusalem in 587 B.C. Jeremiah's function was to assert that because they were the Covenant people they were chastened in the fall; in the Exile they were being shaped on the wheel of suffering; and from the Exile they would reappear in their homeland once again a re-formed vessel, a witness to the faithfulness and goodness of the Covenant God.

Jacob's Day of Distress (30:4-9)

The anguish of the people under judgment is presented in graphic metaphors as the prophet recalls the horrors of the siege and fall: the cry of panic and terror, men's faces pale, their hands clutching their loins like a woman in labor. This was, indeed, a time of distress for Jacob. But a brighter prospect was in view, for the Covenant people were to be saved. In the coming deliverance the Lord would break the yoke of oppression from off their neck, he would burst their bonds. Strangers would no longer make them their servants, for now they would really serve the Lord their God and honor the King whom God would raise up on the throne of David.

Jacob to Be Saved from Afar (30:10-11)

This prophet, like another prophet of the Captivity (Isa. 43: 5-7), reminded the dismayed people that God was really with them. Therefore they were not to fear. One glowing promise is added to another to emphasize God's faithfulness to his people even under judgment. According to the prophet, the divine judgments which permanently leveled other nations were designed to correct Israel, and so to bring God's people to their appointed end. Thus the Covenant people were told not to be dismayed at their present plight because he who chastened them was also with them to save!

Zion's Health Is to Be Restored (30:12-17)

The exiles were reminded now that the present desperate condition of Zion had been brought about by their own sins. If Zion were really left without divine corrective treatment, this condition could well be final. It is as though they were asked, "Who will minister to your condition now? Who will uphold you now? Who can heal you now? What medicine can really heal Israel's wounds?" Israel's "lovers" had forgotten her. Her enemies had dealt her a merciless blow. Her guilt was great because her sins were flagrant. Therefore they were asked, "Why do you cry out over your hurt?" Nevertheless, Zion's God was faithful and he now came forward as a divine Physician to give health and healing. As a sign to the nations that Zion was not an outcast, the nations who consumed her would be consumed. Then no longer could it be said, "It is Zion, for whom no one cares!"

Jerusalem Shall Be Rebuilt (30:18-22)

Jerusalem indeed was in ruins. The word of the Lord had come to pass in overwhelming judgment. But the word of the same Lord was now proclaimed in order to reveal his compassion. Therefore the fortunes of the tents of Jacob were to be restored, and the future could hold out real hope. Jerusalem would be rebuilt. The joys of common life would be expressed in songs of thanksgiving and by the voices of those who make merry. The children of the returning exiles would be multiplied and they would dwell in security. A prince would be raised up from within the congregation of the faithful who would be granted free access to the divine throne. Thus provision would be made for harmony between God and the people (vs. 22; compare Hosea 2:23).

The Intents of the Lord (30:23—31:1)

No passage in the whole book sums up its essential message more faithfully than this twofold affirmation. As a whirling tempest God's wrath had gone forth upon the head of the wicked nation (see 23:19-20). The latter days would usher in the dawn of a bright future when the Lord would be recognized as the God of all the families of Israel. Thus the intents of the Lord would be proclaimed by his mighty acts.

"Grace in the wilderness" (31:2-6)

It is necessary for the reader to distinguish in chapter 31 how the attention is shifted from one type of hearer to another. All the families of Israel are addressed first (31:1-14); then Israel, as Ephraim (vss. 15-22); then Judah (vss. 23-26); and finally the house of Israel and the house of Judah together (vss. 27-40).

The language of verse 2 is reminiscent of an early prophecy of Jeremiah as recorded in 2:2-7. Like his predecessor Hosea, Jeremiah proclaimed God's steadfast love for his people in terms of the marriage bond. God had bound himself to his people by delivering them from Egypt. He had led them through the wilderness. He gave them their good land. Now the same God proclaimed his steadfast love to his scattered people. He had loved them with an everlasting love. Captive Israel had indeed found grace in the wilderness, and this betokened a return to the homeland to be rebuilt. Once again established in her own land, the

Virgin Israel would celebrate the customary festivals. Vineyards would be planted, and in due course she would enjoy the fruit thereof. Glad pilgrimages would be made when the voice of the prophets ("watchmen") was heard.

"He who scattered ... will gather" (31:7-14)

The hosts of returning Israel are invited to rejoice in the God who has proved himself to be the father of his people. He promises to gather them from distant places. Among them will be even the blind and the lame, the woman with child, and the woman in travail. He will guide them unerringly by brooks of water and in a straight path. The reference to Northern Israel as Ephraim is in keeping with the practice of the prophets after this tribe became the recognized leader of the ten tribes (for example, see Hosea 4:17; 5:3-14; Isa. 7:2-9).

To all the nations the glorious restoration of God's people is to be announced. Laments of woe will give place to loud singing on the height of Zion as priests and people alike are satisfied with the goodness of the Lord.

"There is hope for your future" (31:15-22)

Rachel, the mother of Joseph, and so the grandmother of the people of Ephraim and Manasseh now in captivity, is represented as weeping bitterly over her children lost long since in the Assyrian captivity of 721 B.C. By their restoration to their own borders it is affirmed that she will be recompensed. After this manner this passage is usually interpreted. But another view is possible. According to 40:1-6 Jeremiah was released by Nebuzaradan, the Babylonian captain of the guard at Ramah in Benjamin, where he had been kept as a prisoner ever since the fall of Jerusalem. Among his fellow prisoners now on their way into captivity in Babylon there must have been many Benjamites (also descended from Rachel). It has been suggested that this word of the Lord came to Jeremiah at the very spot where these children of Rachel were being torn from her bosom. Her weeping therefore is not to be projected into the imaginary past. And the words of comfort, "Keep your voice from weeping, and your eyes from tears. . . . There is hope for your future," are designed to have a realistic bearing on an actual current situation. They open up before the stricken captives the hope of a return from the land of the enemy. Thus interpreted, the travail of Rachel, whose tomb was near Ramah, was to be justified when her children (these very Benjamites) would come back to their own country.

In 31:18-20 chastened Ephraim (Israel), who had rebelled like a young untamed bullock, is pictured as repenting of his waywardness and pleading for restoration. The ambiguity of this passage is heightened by the lack of any historical point of reference. But such expressions as "I smote upon my thigh" (indicating extreme grief) and "I was ashamed, and I was confounded," seem to indicate that the repentance spoken of is introduced as a condition of restoration rather than an actual experience of penitence on the part of captive Israel. Furthermore, the words that follow—"Is Ephraim my dear son?"—represent God as a father earnestly yearning over his dearly beloved child, adding immeasurably to the force of his entreaty.

Captive Israel, like a backsliding daughter in futile search for a way out of trouble, is urged to set her heart toward the true road homeward by giving due attention to the way which she had taken into captivity (31:21). No satisfactory explanation has ever been offered for the latter part of verse 22, but the sense apparently is that in some way the natural order of things shall be reversed for the better. Whereas the Hebrew text at this place reads, "A woman protects a man," the Greek translation reads, "With safety men may walk about." Thus read, the prophet would be saying: "Israel need not press her search any further, for God has already provided for her safety." There is therefore real hope for her future.

"The land of Judah . . . I will replenish" (31:23-26)

After the coming fortunes of Israel have been predicted, the land of Judah is addressed. Her fortunes, too, are to be restored. Once again justice will flourish. The inhabitants of Judah—city dwellers, farmers, and shepherds alike—will dwell together as a single community, for the weary soul will be satisfied and every languishing soul will be replenished.

The meaning of verse 26 is obscure, but the prophet may be referring to the encouraging character of the preceding vision. Dreams were regarded as an authentic mode of divine communication, and in this case the prophet awoke from his dream refreshed.

"I will sow the house of Israel and ... Judah with ... seed" (31:27-28)

The remaining parts of chapter 31 are addressed significantly to the house of Israel and to the house of Judah together, thus including both branches of the Covenant people as though they were one. This comprehensive form of address becomes all the more significant when the unconditional character of the divine promises made to the one Covenant people is recognized. The exiles are promised first that their land now in ruin is to be repeopled (vss. 27-28).

"Every one shall die for his own sin" (31:29-30)

The popular proverb which appears in 31:29 is quoted by Ezekiel in order to modify it greatly (Ezek. 18:1-32). This is an indication that widespread skepticism must have existed among the exiles. They had witnessed the collapse of Judah as a state. They had suffered the loss of goods and loved ones. They had been deported into almost intolerable physical conditions. It was no wonder that these exiles had sunk into bitter disillusionment. Rather than admit the justice of their present plight as a stark and inevitable consequence of their own sins, they apparently were quoting this proverb to shift the blame onto others, as though they, innocent children, were now suffering for the sins of their parents.

Jeremiah quotes the proverb as he points to a new order in human affairs, one that applies with special relevance to the Covenant people. Henceforth this popular form of the proverb can no longer be quoted. Henceforth every individual must regard himself as accountable to God personally: "Each man who eats sour grapes, his teeth shall be set on edge."

One can easily recognize how the original proverb could have had validity in a former day when the sense of corporate solidarity united a whole family in responsibility for an act like that of Achan (Joshua, ch. 7). But now the exiles are apparently assuming that the Creator was acting unnaturally in transferring guilt from parents to children. The prophet meets such an insinuation by a momentous forecast. The validity of the proverb itself as a principle of action in the past is left unchallenged (in Deut. 24:16 it had been challenged). Instead, a new order of ethical responsibility before God is announced, "Every one shall die for his own sin." In such a context as this the high point of the Book of Jeremiah is reached. His most important single teaching now is introduced precisely where the ethical significance of the new divine order is most singularly stressed.

The New Covenant (31:31-34)

One of the most overlooked features of this passage is the expression, "says the LORD," repeated four times (vss. 31, 32, 33, 34). When the force of this expression is clearly recognized, the passage is lifted into mountain-peak significance as seen from the broader perspective of biblical revelation. The words "says the LORD" in English fail to do justice to the Hebrew text, which suggests that the prophet is in intimate converse with God, as though he were receiving from him, by whisper, a secret message of revelation. The repeated expression, "says," may more forcibly be translated, "utters." So then the four-times-repeated "utters the LORD," or "utterance of the LORD," suggests that the prophet records what he receives as it is revealed to him. Thus these words are stamped with singular authority. And the intimate connection, theologically, of this prophecy with the preceding emphasis on individual responsibility, suggests that Jeremiah's words, as recorded here, give an authentic and glowing answer to the sullen skepticism of the Covenant people now in exile.

A second characteristic looms large in the language of this significant pronouncement. The verbs, "I will make," "I will put," "I will write," "I will be," "I will forgive," all emphasize the fact that the Covenant God is taking the initiative here. If Jeremiah spoke these words while the taste of defeat and deportation was still bitter in the mouths of his countrymen, what he said had an even more direct bearing upon their urgent need for an authentic word from God. What could prevent hot, cynical words from escaping their lips? The Holy City was in ruins. The Temple was destroyed. The Ark of the Covenant was gone. Was God really impotent as some had suggested? Was he actually indifferent to their plight? Had he not broken his Covenant with them? Spoken to such a mood, the language glows with truth and light. "No, the exact opposite is the case," declares the prophet. God really cares for his people. It is they and their fathers who have persistently broken the Covenant ever since it was made at Sinai at the time when God delivered his people from bondage in Egypt.

The words "though I was their husband" (vs. 32) can also be translated "although I was a Lord over them." Like his predecessor Hosea, Jeremiah had pictured God's Covenant in terms of the marriage bond (2:2; 3:6-14). Now he reaffirmed that in the Covenant at Sinai, God had taken possession of his people as a husband does a bride. Thus he stressed the essential relation between God and the people as a personal one based upon mutual affection. Meanwhile God had been faithful to his people even though they had broken the Covenant. Now, however, God was initiating something new. The force of the word translated "But" in verse 33 introduces a strong contrast: "Nay, to the contrary. God has not forsaken his people." God comes to them now not as requiring, but as offering. The old Covenant could not suffice any longer. It could not be patched up. Instead God was now at hand to make promises to his people—better promises, in fact, than he had made before. This initiative on the part of God was recognized by the author of the Letter to the Hebrews. Before he proceeded to expound the priestly work of Christ as the minister of a new Covenant, he quoted this passage from Jeremiah, to show that "the covenant he mediates is better, since it is enacted on better promises" (Heb. 8:6-13).

Still a third feature of this passage stands out when proper recognition is given to the word "new." The Covenant which God now proposes is conceived to be new not in its substance but in its springs of action. The house of Israel and the house of Judah are still the Covenant people. God's promise, "I will be their God, and they shall be my people," is just as valid as it was before. But the conditions by which this blessed relationship can be nurtured and maintained effectively in action are new. Formerly, under the Covenant, the people were called upon to obey the Law, but God's Law as a code did not elicit a spontaneous response on the part of the people. Being something external, "thou shalt," "thou shalt not," it could only urge or prohibit certain kinds of action. It could not cleanse or stir the springs of action. Consequently, although God had taken their fathers "by the hand," though he had plighted his troth to them as a husband, they and their fathers had broken away. The time was coming when the conditions of fellowship with God were to be made real and effective in action. Three better promises therefore are made to the faltering Covenant people.

The first promise is "I will put my law [Torah, "instruction"] within them." What is written on one's heart suggests mutuality of affection. It implies a union of wills. If God's claims entered into a person's understanding as an expression of God's will, the individual could respond spontaneously, without being burdened by any external commands.

The second promise is, "They shall all know me." This gracious promise points directly to the individual aspects of the new Covenant. Firsthand, intuitive knowledge can never be "taught." It must be grasped, or "caught." Some kinds of knowledge can be learned by rote or taught as precepts. So under the old Covenant one man could cause his neighbor to learn the Law (vs. 34). But such an external knowledge of God and his ways could never induce corresponding action; the neighbor could "take it or leave it." But in the future a new principle of action was to be put into force. Henceforth God's promises would be written upon their hearts.

The third promise, "I will forgive their iniquity, and I will remember their sin no more," makes such a relation both potent and effective. To have the burden of guilt removed, to be absolved from failure, to be set free—all this gives the forgiven person a new sense of worth. And with this sense of worth comes the desire to be really worthy. In the whole human universe, what force has greater regenerative potency? What else has such power to stir the springs of ethical action? By being grounded in God's everlasting grace to forgive, both the potency and the permanence of the new Covenant are assured.

Finally, it would be too much to say that Jeremiah saw all this clearly or that he expected the Covenant people to understand it clearly. He and they alike saw through a glass darkly. But Jeremiah recognized God's promises afar off. He saw the essential character of the new Covenant. He saw that God is gracious. Therefore he could cry with confidence, "Behold, the days are coming, says the LORD." No mountain peak, however isolated, exists unto itself alone, for there are always other peaks, distant though they may be. As every mountain peak stands within a larger setting, so does this passage. No interpreter of these words will do justice to Jeremiah's prediction of the new Covenant unless he sees this Covenant in the total biblical setting where peak can be seen in relation to peak.

Within the scope of such a view there are at least three significant points of reference:

First of all, it is because of this passage in Jeremiah that the two parts of the Holy Bible are called The Old Covenant (Testament) and The New Covenant (Testament). This distinction between the two Covenants (or Testaments) was developed by Paul in his Second Letter to the Corinthians, where he speaks of the Books of the Law ("Moses"), when they are read in the synagogue, as "the old covenant" (II Cor. 3:14-16), and where he refers to the Apostles as "ministers of a new covenant" (II Cor. 3:6). By the end of the second century the Church Fathers were making general use of these terms in relation to the two parts of the Bible.

Second, the author of the Letter to the Hebrews begins and ends his exposition of the high priestly ministry of Jesus Christ by quoting from Jeremiah 31:31-34. The Covenant he mediates is better, so the Letter to the Hebrews declares, "since it is enacted on better promises. For if that first covenant had been faultless, there would have been no occasion for a second" (8:6-7). And he concludes his exposition by quoting the words of Jeremiah 31:34, adding, "Where there is forgiveness of these, there is no longer any offering for sin" (Heb. 10:17-18).

Third, these words of Jeremiah lie behind the words of the institution of the Lord's Supper. Thus Paul declares that he received from the Lord what he also delivered to the church at Corinth (I Cor. 11:23-26). And Jesus himself, before he went to the Cross, while celebrating the Passover with his disciples on the night he was betrayed, gave solemn and significant meaning to Jeremiah's words. Having broken the bread, he took the cup and gave thanks and said, "This is my blood of the covenant, which is poured out for many" (Mark 14:24; see Exod. 24:8; also Matt. 26:26-29).

"Israel . . . for ever" (31:35-37)

As though to back up with still further assurance the momentous utterance of the Lord concerning the new Covenant, a passage which proclaims his faithfulness as seen in "the fixed order" of nature is added here. If this fixed order, the sun for light by day, the moon and the stars for light by night, should depart, then would the descendants of Israel cease. Furthermore, if the heavens above could be measured, or if the foundations of the earth below could be explored, then would the descendants of Israel be cast off "for all that they have done." Preaching like this must have exerted a telling influence upon the exiles to make them aware of the unlimited scope of God's word of forgiveness.

"The city ... rebuilt" (31:38-40)

A final utterance of the Lord, prefaced by the same words as the proclamation of the new Covenant, "Behold, the days are coming," concludes chapter 31. "The city shall be rebuilt for the LORD." While some of the references in this passage are obscure, such as "the hill Gareb," and "Goah," the most striking expression in the passage is "for the LORD." The city is to be rebuilt *for the Lord*. Jerusalem has been built, destroyed, rebuilt, destroyed, rebuilt! What other historic city has a biography at all comparable to that of Jerusalem? The words "It shall not be uprooted or overthrown any more for ever" seem at first to be strange. Cities like Nineveh and Babylon, under divine judgment, were uprooted and overthrown forever. But Jerusalem is "sacred to the LORD" (31:40), even under judgment. Jerusalem somehow always has been raised up from its ashes to be rebuilt, not because the city has been at all true to its name, but because it is "sacred to the LORD . . . for ever." "On the holy mount stands the city he founded" (Ps. 87:1).

Jeremiah in the Court of the Guard (32:1-5)

The narrative which introduces chapter 32 is closely connected with the events related in 37:11-21. Jeremiah was now a prisoner in the court of the guard (compare 32:2 with 37:21 and 38:1-28). The siege which had begun in the ninth year of Zedekiah (589 B.C.) had been under way now for some time (32:1, "in the tenth year of Zedekiah"). Meanwhile the king and the prophet had been in touch with each other repeatedly. Four times Jeremiah had delivered the word of the Lord to Zedekiah (21:1-7; 34:1-7; 37:16-21; 38:14-28). The weak king seems to have been hoping secretly for some miraculous deliverance. Jeremiah, plainly and boldly, had told the king that he would not escape out of the hand of the Chaldeans (32:4). "You shall surely be captured," he was saying, "and delivered into the hand of the king of Babylon; you shall see the king of Babylon eye to eye and speak with him face to face, and you shall go to Babylon." Jeremiah had been put into the miry pit, but he had been rescued and returned as a prisoner to the court of the guard which was located in the royal palace (38:7-28).

Hanamel said, "Buy my field" (32:6-8)

During an unexpected lull in the siege, Jeremiah had sought to leave the city and go to Anathoth concerning some family matter ("to receive his portion there among the people," 37:12). But instead he had been arrested as a deserter, and had been flogged and imprisoned. He had been prevented from performing some family duty (the Hebrew text of 37:12 is obscure). Now that he was imprisoned and could not go to Anathoth, would someone come to him?

This passage is instructive in two significant ways. First, it illuminates how Jeremiah recognized what was to him "the word of the LORD." We read, "The word of the LORD came to me: Behold, Hanamel the son of Shallum your uncle will come to you and say, 'Buy my field'" (32:6-7). We also read, "Then Hanamel my cousin came . . . and said to me, 'Buy my field'" (32:8). Finally we read, "Then I knew that this was the word of the LORD." The close sequence in this learning experience is remarkable: Jeremiah attempted to go to Anathoth; he was prevented. He had a presentiment, which he identified as the word of the Lord, that his cousin would come to him. He came. He used words identical with "the word of the LORD." Jeremiah concluded, "Then I knew." But the subsequent actions are equally instructive: "I bought the field" (32:9); "I prayed" (32:16). Second, this passage illustrates the law of redemption of land by which property rights were kept within families (Lev. 25:25-28; Ruth 3:6—4:12). Had Jeremiah attempted to go to Anathoth for this purpose? At any rate, the right of possession and redemption was his.

"And I bought the field" (32:9-15)

The exactness of the detail in which this unusual transaction is recorded is remarkable. The specified price, the weighing of money, the signing of the deed in the presence of witnesses, the open and the sealed copies, the signing of the witnesses, the onlooking crowd, the deposit of both documents in an earthenware vessel, the declared meaning of the action, and the available resources of the prisoner taken all together make this one of the most fascinating episodes in the whole book. But the account derives special interest from the fact that the land was purchased at the very time when the whole surrounding country was in enemy hands. This act on the part of the prophet was no mere investment; it had unusual symbolic significance. It dramatized eloquently Jeremiah's confidence in the future of his people and in their sure return to their homeland, "For thus says the LORD of hosts, the God of Israel: Houses and fields and vineyards shall again be bought in this land" (32:15).

"I prayed to the Lord, saying ..." (32:16-25)

The extraordinary act of purchasing land which was his by right of redemption but at present was in enemy hands weighed heavily upon the prophet, and he sought relief in prayer. His words, "What thou didst speak has come to pass" (32:24), may have a double meaning. They may mean that the word of the Lord concerning the offer of Hanamel had taken place, and that Jeremiah had acted accordingly. They could also mean that the word of the Lord about the Chaldean war on Judah had come to pass. This is probably the most direct meaning, for the prophet adds, "Behold, thou seest it." Then he unburdens his soul: "Yet thou, O Lord GOD, hast said to me, 'Buy the field for money and get witnesses'—though the city is given into the hands of the Chaldeans" (32:24-25). The prayer attributed here to the prophet is as remarkable as the event with which it is associated. God is addressed first as the Creator, for whom nothing is too hard. He is the providential Arbiter of the ways of all men. He is the Redeemer and gracious Benefactor of the Covenant people. Yet they, like their fathers, did not obey his voice nor heed his commandments. The siege mounds raised against the city, the sword, famine, and pestilence, all bore witness that what the Lord had spoken had really come to pass. The mood of Jeremiah as expressed in these words is characteristic of the way he had received and proclaimed God's word throughout his ministry. The sigh of the prophet, "Ah Lord GOD!" which introduces the prayer is echoed in the "Yet" at the end of the prayer, as though a correspondingly satisfying answer were desired. The answer to the prophet's expressed desire is recorded in the words which follow.

"The word of the Lord came to Jeremiah" (32:26-44)

The answer to Jeremiah's prayer begins on the same note as that on which the prayer itself had begun, but in the form of a question, "Is anything too hard for me?" The Hebrew word

translated "hard" really means "wonderful." It is used in Isaiah
as an attribute of deity (28:29; see also 29:14; 9:6) and in the
Psalms to refer to his works (40:5). God is said to act in accordance with his nature, consequently his actions are declared to be
"wonderful." The answer given to Jeremiah's prayer recorded in
32:16-25 is twofold.

First, the Holy City had come under judgment indeed. It was
about to be taken by the Chaldeans, who would set it on fire and
burn it with the houses on whose roofs incense had been offered
to Baal. The sons of Israel and Judah were guilty on four counts:
Their idolatry had been widespread and deliberate (vss. 29-32);
they had obdurately resisted divine instruction (vs. 33); they
had defiled the Temple by setting up abominations in it (vs. 34);
they had caused Judah to sin by offering up sons and daughters
to Molech at the high place in the valley of the son of Hinnom
(vs. 35).

Second, the restoration of the Holy City was sure. True to his
name, the God of Israel would gather his people from their captivity and bring them back to their homeland securely (vss. 37-
38). Being their God he would give them another heart to fear
him (vs. 39). He would make with them an everlasting Covenant
to do them good (vss. 40-41). Just as he had judged them by
hurling them from their land, so he would restore the land to
them that fields again might be bought, deeds might be sub-
scribed and sealed and witnessed (vss. 42-44), as indicated in
the symbolic purchase of the Anathoth field.

Health and Restoration Are Promised to Judah (33:1-26)

The Book of Consolation (chs. 30-33) is now concluded by
utterances which, like those of the preceding chapters, reiterate
the contrasted themes of judgment and restoration without any
attempt to specify a definite chronological setting except at the
beginning. According to 33:1, Jeremiah was still a prisoner in
the court of the guard. Meanwhile (vs. 4), to provide materials
of defense against the besiegers certain houses in the city had
been torn down. (See Isaiah 22:9-10 for a similar example when
Jerusalem was under siege over a century before.) The fall of
Jerusalem could not have been far distant (vs. 5) when this
word of the Lord came to Jeremiah (33:1-9). The remainder of
chapter 33 was composed after the city had fallen. The land is
described as waste and the streets of Jerusalem as desolate (vs.

10). The cities of Judah are depopulated (vs. 12), as well as those of the hill country (north of Jerusalem), of the Shephelah (west), and of the Negeb (south). The closing utterances suggest a time later on in the Captivity when some of the exiles, in deep discouragement, had concluded that the Lord had rejected his people altogether. Chapter 33 therefore is a fitting conclusion to the "Book of Consolation."

The first section (33:1-9) provides a snapshot of the prophet's thoughts when the fall of the city was imminent. Amid the feverish tensions which immediately preceded the fall of the city, and the accompanying distress of famine, pestilence, and death which stalked all about him, the prophet himself had barely escaped from death in the miry pit (38:7-13). Under such desperate conditions the invitation (33:3) to call upon the name of the Lord, the Creator, for instruction concerning his hidden but gracious designs is all the more remarkable. In such a mood two unshakable certainties seized upon the mind of the prophet. First (33:8), guilty Judah was suffering for her ingrained sin (her deviation from a clearly marked course), and for her willful rebellion (her deliberate transgressions). From the days of his earliest ministry Jeremiah had been warning his generation against pursuing such a fatal course (compare 2:23-25). Such preaching had been ignored and persistently resisted over Jeremiah's forty-year-long ministry. That he was not disillusioned or depressed now under such circumstances is a glowing tribute to the genuineness of Jeremiah's faith and the reality of his hope. Second, in spite of the severity of this judgment upon Judah's guilt, another certainty glowed in Jeremiah's mind (33:6-9). In fact, it overbalanced the immediate consequence of Judah's guilt. Although at present God had hidden his face from this city, he proposed to bring to it "health and healing . . . prosperity and security." The city which had failed in its vocation so completely would be forgiven all its guilt. This passage, therefore, in spite of the difficulties presented by the condition of the Hebrew text (see the margin of the Revised Standard Version) sounds forth the two emphatic notes which are so characteristic of the Book of Consolation. Sinful Judah must be judged. The fortunes of chastened Judah are to be restored.

It is clear that 33:10-13 was composed after the fall of the Holy City. All of Judah and the surrounding country, north, west, and south, was waste and desolate. Sinful Judah was suffering for all her sins. However, a different prospect came into view. In accordance with his unshakable hope in God's goodness (33:9), the repopulation of Jerusalem was envisaged by the prophet. This blessing would be accompanied by the restoration of normal human relationships and the renewal of undisturbed pastoral security in the land. These aspects of the restoration of Judah's fortunes correspond to a similar emphasis in the Book of Consolation found in 30:19 and 31:4, 12-14.

Certain critical problems face the interpreter of Jeremiah 33: 14-26. These verses are completely lacking in the Greek translation of the Book of Jeremiah. Is this because the translator did not find this passage in his Hebrew text? Or could the translator have failed to include it? The latter could hardly be possible in the case of a passage which abounds so fully with glowing promises. The promises made in the successive parts of this passage are strikingly similar to corresponding promises made elsewhere in the book. The promise of the righteous Branch in 33:14-16 is parallel to that in 23:5-6. The language "never lack a man" used twice in 33:17-18 is parallel to the same expression in 35:19. The references to day and night and the heavens and the earth are used to apply, with slight variations, to the descendants of Israel in both 33:20-26 and 31:35-36.

The content of 33:14-26, while showing striking similarity to other passages in the book, is nevertheless distinctive enough to have been given a special place in the Book of Consolation as it was being organized into its present form. It appears to have been added here because of its hopeful character, from prophetic materials which during the Exile were gathered about the work and messages of Jeremiah.

First of all, God's faithfulness to the Covenant people is reasserted. In due course, so it is promised, God will raise up the true offspring of David (a righteous "Branch," literally Sprout or Shoot; compare Isa. 4:2; Jer. 23:5), who will reign with justice and righteousness. Here, however, the Messianic name, "The LORD is our righteousness," is applied to the city of Jerusalem, as the community of the faithful, rather than to a single individual in the person of the Messianic King (33:14-16).

Second, it is proclaimed that in the new divine order God will make good his word never to cut off a true successor to the throne of David or a priesthood from offering sacrifices continually. The expression "shall never lack a man" used twice in verses 17 and

18 is hardly meant to refer to a whole line of kings or priests. Rather it guarantees that the office of king and priest is to be perpetual. Furthermore, this guarantee is to be as sure in its working as the succession of day and night (33:19-22).

Third, both Israel and Judah were now in a sorry plight as despised exiles. Nevertheless it is asserted that God's Covenant with them still stands. He has not cast off his Chosen People. Though day and night should cease, though the ordinances of heaven and earth should fail, still he would not reject the descendants of Jacob or the house of David (33:23-26).

The Slaves Freed, Then Re-enslaved (34:1-22)

Chapter 34 consists of two parts. According to verses 1-7 the Babylonian army under Nebuchadnezzar had invaded Palestine. Only Jerusalem and two other fortified cities, Lachish and Azekah, remained untaken. Jeremiah offered urgent counsel to Zedekiah. The remainder of the chapter deals with the act of the citizens of Jerusalem, who, at the direction of the king, had released their slaves and sealed their compact with solemn ceremonies. When the Egyptian army advanced from the south to relieve the pressure on Jerusalem, the Babylonian army temporarily withdrew (see 37:1-10). Promptly the owners of the slaves cancelled their compact. For this breach of faith Jeremiah proclaimed that the Babylonians would return to the city and take it.

Jeremiah Counsels with Zedekiah (34:1-7)

Jeremiah never compromised his position regarding Judah's relations to Babylon. When once Nebuchadnezzar had deported Jehoiachin and the ten thousand chief people; when he had appointed Mattaniah as king of Judah and changed his name to Zedekiah; and when Zedekiah in turn had given an oath of allegiance to Nebuchadnezzar, Jeremiah insisted that Zedekiah wear the yoke of the king of Babylon "and serve him and his people, and live" (Jer. 27:12-15; see II Kings 24:1-17). Furthermore, he had already warned that to join a conspiracy with other nations against Babylon would be futile (27:1-11). But Zedekiah broke his oath and allied himself with Egypt (Ezek. 17:13-21). In 589 B.C., Nebuchadnezzar invaded Palestine. Jeremiah then counseled Zedekiah to surrender without further resistance (21:1-7).

As fighting in Judah continued, the pressure against Jerusalem was increasing. Jeremiah affirmed that the city would be taken and burned. He announced that Zedekiah, too, would surely be captured. He would have to answer for his past conduct "eye to eye" and "face to face." He would not be slain, but would be taken captive to Babylon where he would die and be accorded the customary rites. At this time, besides Jerusalem, only Lachish (Tell ed-Duweir, about 23 miles southwest of Jerusalem) and Azekah (some 11 miles northeast of Lachish) remained untaken among all the fortified cities of Judah. Excavations at Lachish reveal how completely it was destroyed at this time. Letters written on broken pieces of pottery called sherds were discovered there in 1935. These letters reflect how disturbed the condition of the country was just before the final destruction of Lachish at the end of Zedekiah's reign. One of these sherds, which must have been carried by a courier from an outpost to an officer in Lachish, reads, "We are watching for the smoke-signals of Lachish according to all the instructions which my lord gave, because we cannot see the signals of Azekah." This sherd (Letter Number Four), found in the ashes of Lachish, gives striking confirmation of the words in 34:6-7.

Liberty to the Slaves Proclaimed and Revoked (34:8-11)

While the Babylonian armies were tightening their grip on the land of Judah, Zedekiah directed the people to proclaim liberty to their Hebrew slaves. The motives for this action doubtless were mixed. Would freed slaves join more heartily in the defense of the city? Would their former masters be relieved from feeding them? Would the renewal of this practice of freeing slaves, which had apparently long been disregarded, be pleasing to God? In any case, the compact with the slaves was sealed by solemn ceremonies. The words of verse 11, "But afterward," are significant. According to 37:1-10 and 34:21-22, there was a lull in the siege. The Egyptian armies from the south, presumably relieving Jerusalem, drew the Babylonian forces away from the besieged city. Once again slaves could work in the fields outside the city. Military pressure against the city was relieved. Was the trouble over? The freed slaves were re-enslaved.

Liberty to the Sword Proclaimed (34:12-22)

According to Deuteronomy 15:12-15 (compare Exod. 21:2-

11), no Hebrew was to enslave a brother Hebrew permanently. He might use his brother's services only for a period of six years, then he must set him free. This practice had been neglected (34: 14). But now the people had "repented" and sealed their action by solemn rites in the Temple (vs. 15). In performing these rites the people of Jerusalem, including their princes, priests, and other leaders, had passed between the parts of a calf which had been cut in two (a sacrificial rite, associated with Covenant ceremonies; compare Gen. 15:7-17). Thus in "cutting this covenant" the people of Jerusalem had proclaimed their readiness to be treated as this sacred victim. Jeremiah denounced them for their breach of faith. They not only had done a wrong to their fellow Hebrews, they also had profaned the divine name (vs. 16). Let them hear the word of the Lord: "Behold, I proclaim to you liberty to the sword, to pestilence, and to famine" (vs. 17). Zedekiah and his princes would be given into the hand of their enemies. The Babylonian armies would surely return to the city and take it. Jerusalem would become desolate without inhabitant.

The Fidelity of the Rechabites (35:1-19)

To prick the conscience of the Covenant people for their infidelity, Jeremiah used many pointed illustrations. Some examples may be recalled. "Has a nation changed its gods . . .? But my people . . ." (2:11); "Have I been a wilderness to Israel . . .? Why then do my people say . . .?" (2:31); "Can a maiden forget her ornaments . . .? Yet my people . . ." (2:32); "Even the stork in the heavens . . . but my people . . ." (8:7); "Do the mountain waters run dry . . .? But my people . . ." (18:14-15). Jeremiah now found a singular example of filial constancy in the Rechabites, and he planned a bold way in which to dramatize it in order to convict the men of Judah. "The sons of Jonadab the son of Rechab have kept the command which their father gave them, but this people . . ." (35:16).

Chapter 35 is undated, but the reference to the army of the Chaldeans and the army of the Syrians in 35:11 indicates that the events here described probably occurred in the reign of Jehoiakim sometime after the battle of Carchemish (605 B.C.), when Nebuchadnezzar sent guerilla bands against the rebellious Jehoiakim (II Kings 24:1-2). Chapter 35 clearly has no historical connection with chapter 34. Certain parallels between the language of chapters 35 and 36, however, may account for the position of chapter 35 at this place in the book.

Jeremiah Sets Wine Before the Rechabites (35:1-5)

The Rechabites were a nomadic tribe of Kenite descent (I Chron. 2:55). They traced their practices to Jonadab (Jehonadab) the son of Rechab, whose zeal for the true worship of the Lord led him to support Jehu in his suppression of the house of Ahab (II Kings 10:15-24). Jonadab had feared the entanglements of a settled life. He wanted to preserve the primitive simplicity of life in the desert as a protest against the corruptions of Baal worship. He commanded his family and their descendants to dwell in tents, to abstain from wine and all strong drink, to sow no seed, and to plant no vineyard. It was not their mode of life but the motive behind their living which attracted Jeremiah to the Rechabites at this time. Having been driven into Jerusalem from the desert by the guerilla raids of the Chaldeans and Syrians, this tribe provided Jeremiah with a timely opportunity to impress an object lesson of fidelity upon his countrymen.

Jeremiah brought certain Rechabites including Jaazaniah, probably their leader, into a chamber within the Temple court (compare Jer. 36:10, 20) where they might be seen by Temple officials and others. Although no significance seems to be attached to the particular chambers of the Temple court mentioned, the care given to such details as the position of the chambers and the names of their occupants adds both to the interest and to the value of the narrative. Jeremiah set pitchers of wine and wine cups before the Rechabites and urged them, "Drink wine" (vs. 5).

The Rechabites Refuse to Drink (35:6-11)

The Rechabites not only refused to drink, they gave voluble reasons for their practice of abstinence. They recited why and how they lived as they did, summing it up in their words: "We have obeyed the voice of Jonadab the son of Rechab, our father, in all that he commanded us." Their strict adherence to an ancient command spoke for itself. The only reason they were in Jerusalem at all was to find security for the present while the countryside was invaded.

The Lesson for Judah (35:12-19)

The lesson to be drawn from the Rechabites' refusal to drink

wine was obvious. Here were men who obeyed restraints placed
upon them by an ancestor long since dead. Yet the men of Judah,
although they had been warned persistently by the prophets, had
failed to heed the commandments of the living God. Once again
the familiar words, "Turn . . . and . . . dwell," were heard in the
Temple courts. This had been the theme of Jeremiah's Temple
Sermon (7:1-15). This same note had been made emphatic when
Jeremiah reviewed his prophetic messages at the time of the
battle of Carchemish (25:1-7). This message would be proclaimed
again when Baruch read the scroll at the time of a fast in the
Temple court (36:1-8). To Jeremiah, heedless impenitence was
inexcusable. To persist in such a course was fatal. It could only
bring evil consequences upon Judah and Jerusalem (35:17).

To the Rechabites, however, a brighter prospect was in view.
Because they had kept all the precepts of their ancient father,
Jonadab would "never lack a man" to stand before the Lord.
Their tribute as a living example of filial devotion would be
pleasing to the Lord as a service forever.

Jeremiah and the Two Scrolls (36:1-32)

Chapter 36 is one of the most important passages in the whole
book. In the annals of prophetic writing it is unique. Nowhere
else is it shown with such elaborate attention to detail how the
word of the Lord to a man of God came to be recorded. This
passage is significant also for its emphasis upon the hazardous
nature of Jeremiah's prophetic work. Furthermore this passage
marks a turning point in Jeremiah's career. Up to this time Jeremiah, within the lifetime of his own generation, was a marked
man. Now, through his writings, he was destined to belong to
all men across the centuries. There is a close relation between
the narrative of chapter 36 and that of chapter 25 since the experiences recorded in both chapters are dated in the same year
and both involve the recording of his prophecies. Other chapters in this book which are dated in the fourth year of Jehoiakim
are chapter 45 (which should be read between the lines of 36:8
and 9), and 46:2-12.

Jeremiah Dictates the First Scroll (36:1-7)

Having failed to stir up the people to repentance by his previous discourses at the Temple (26:1-19; 7:1-15; 19:14-15),

Jeremiah was now moved to commit to writing the word of the Lord which had come to him. Accordingly he dictated his prophecies to Baruch his scribe. Baruch is identified as the son of Neriah here and in 32:9-15. That Baruch came from an important family in Jerusalem is suggested in 51:59, where his brother Seraiah is said to have been sent upon a diplomatic mission to Babylon, in company with Zedekiah. Baruch has been described by Josephus as coming from a very distinguished family and as exceptionally well instructed in his native language. While Jeremiah dictated, his scribe wrote the words upon a scroll. Why Jeremiah was debarred from going into the Temple is not clear, but verse 26 excludes any suggestion of imprisonment, as might be implied from the "shut up" of some English versions. It may be that he was forbidden to appear in the Temple for fear of causing a disturbance (compare ch. 26), or he may have been restrained by some ceremonial hindrance. The strategy of writing out his prophecies so that they could be read to the people who gathered in the Temple on a fast day was a shrewd way of directing their supplications to the Lord toward a very practical end (36:3, 7).

Baruch Reads from the Scroll (36:8, 9-10)

Chapter 45 should be read in connection with 36:8 since the experience recorded there is connected with the composition of the scroll both by date and by circumstance. According to chapter 45, the process of composing the scroll must have been arduous. It was also protracted, for it was not until the fifth year of Jehoiakim, in the ninth month (probably our December), that Baruch read from the finished scroll. The reading took place in the chamber of Gemariah which was in the upper court of the Temple near the New Gate. This is the court where Jeremiah had been put on trial for his life after the Temple Sermon (see 26:10-11).

Baruch Reads the Scroll to the Princes (36:11-19)

The significance of the contents of the scroll is indicated by the reaction of Micaiah the son of Gemariah in whose chamber the scroll was read. What Micaiah heard made such an impression on him that he immediately reported the matter to the princes, whose names indicate that they were responsible Temple officials. These men were gathered in the secretary's chamber in the palace. What follows in the passage is a masterpiece of reporting. The reader is told about the dispatch of Jehudi and the command to Baruch, "Take in your hand the scroll . . . and come." Then the reader hears the words spoken to the scribe, "Sit down and read it." He learns about their fear when they heard, and their decision, "We must report all these words to the king." He hears their query, "How did you write all these words?", and he hears Baruch's answer: "He dictated all these words to me, while I wrote them with ink on the scroll." Finally he reads their words of precaution, "Go and hide, you and Jeremiah, and let no one know where you are."

The Scroll Is Read to the King (36:20-26)

When the matter was reported to Jehoiakim he ordered that the scroll be brought from the chamber of Elishama the secretary and that it be read before him. The reaction of Jehoiakim was characteristic of his highhanded ways (compare 22:13-19). But it was quite in contrast to that of his father Josiah when the Book of the Law was read in his hearing (II Kings 22:8-13). Because it was winter, a fire was burning in the brazier before the king. As Jehudi read a few columns the king cut off that portion of the scroll with a penknife and threw it into the fire. This went on until the whole scroll had been read and consumed, even though some of the princes urged the king not to burn it. Jehoiakim's contemptuous attitude influenced the princes, for it is said that none of those who heard all these words "was afraid, nor did they rend their garments." When the king ordered the arrest of Baruch and Jeremiah, both men were already securely hidden.

Another Scroll Is Written (36:27-32)

How many of Jeremiah's previous prophecies were included in the first scroll is not known. But in hiding, the prophet and his scribe had ample time to enlarge the content of the first scroll in a second scroll which they now set about to compose. In it they included a final warning to Jehoiakim, while to the original words of the first scroll, "many similar words were added." How much of the present Book of Jeremiah we owe to this scroll is uncertain, but it can be safely estimated that much of the content of chapters 1-20 was included in it.

Chapter 36 is invaluable for the light it throws upon the process by which the message of Jeremiah was recorded for posterity.

Jeremiah and the Siege of Jerusalem (37:1—38:28)

An Introductory Heading (37:1-2)

The words of 37:1-2 serve as an introduction to the narrative of chapters 37 and 38, which record events occurring within the eighteen-month siege of Jerusalem (589-587 B.C.). This heading also provides a transition from the narrative of chapter 36, which is dated in the fourth year of the reign of Jehoiakim (605 B.C.).

Zedekiah Requests Jeremiah to Pray (37:3-10)

Other passages have given scattered hints about Jeremiah's activities during the siege of Jerusalem. According to 21:1-10, Zedekiah had asked Jeremiah to intercede with the Lord. His word, "perhaps" (21:2), suggests that Zedekiah had a vain hope that Jerusalem might even yet escape destruction. This passage (21:1-10) is thought by some interpreters to be but a parallel of 37:3-10, but one of the representatives sent by Zedekiah to Jeremiah is different and the essential circumstances are not identical. Meanwhile, Jeremiah had confronted Zedekiah with the unhappy fate which surely awaited him (34:1-7). Also a compact to free the slaves had been proclaimed by solemn rites in the Temple (34:8-10). Now the Babylonian army had temporarily lifted the siege to check the advance of Egyptian troops from the south. Zedekiah, thinking that the lifting of the siege betokened deliverance, sent Jehucal the son of Shelemiah (compare 38:1) and Zephaniah the priest (compare 21:1; 29:25-29; 52:24) to urge Jeremiah: "Pray for us to the LORD our God." Jeremiah promptly predicted that the Egyptian advance was no answer to Jerusalem's predicament. The Chaldean army would come again to besiege the city, and would take it and burn it with fire. To entertain any other hope, Jeremiah declared, would be self-deception (37:9), for the word of the Lord proclaimed the fall of the city.

Jeremiah Is Arrested and Imprisoned (37:11-15)

The withdrawal of the Chaldeans from the city gave Jeremiah an opportunity to go to his parental home in the land of Benjamin. The Gate of Benjamin (possibly the Sheep Gate) was on the north side of the city. Through this gate the road led northward toward Anathoth. As Jeremiah passed through the gate,

Irijah, the officer of the watch, arrested him. Jeremiah was charged with desertion and turned over to the princes (administrative officials). These men, enraged, flogged the prophet and imprisoned him. Since Jeremiah had publicly urged the people to desert (compare 21:8-10), this charge was not entirely groundless. In any case it gave these officials the excuse they wanted to apprehend and imprison Jeremiah on "legal" grounds, and he was placed in the dungeon house (literally, "house of the pit").

Zedekiah Questions Jeremiah Secretly (37:16-21)

Meanwhile the situation in Jerusalem was growing steadily worse. Zedekiah sent for Jeremiah and questioned him secretly in the palace. "Is there any word from the LORD?" he asked. Jeremiah's answer was direct and clear, "There is." He pointed to the futile predictions of Zedekiah's false advisers to the effect that the Chaldeans would not return. Now events themselves had confirmed Jeremiah's warnings. And he added, "You shall be delivered into the hand of the king of Babylon" (37:17). Jeremiah had clear grounds on which to plead for himself. He requested to be released from the dungeon cell in the house of Jonathan. Lest the prophet die in this "house of the pit," the king ordered him to be transferred to the court of the guard within the palace grounds. Here the prophet could have a share in the daily ration of bread brought to the prisoners from the bakers' street. Probably it was shortly after this that the events recorded in chapter 32 occurred.

Jeremiah Is Rescued from the Cistern (38:1-13)

Since the court of the guard was in the royal palace, it was used to confine prisoners who were under the immediate jurisdiction of the king (compare Neh. 3:25). Their confinement was semipublic. Hanamel, Jeremiah's cousin, came here to request Jeremiah to purchase the field at Anathoth, and here the transaction was carried out (32:1-15). Furthermore, Jeremiah took advantage of this opportunity to keep in touch with the public, and urged the people to desert to the Chaldeans. He promised that anyone who did so could thereby save his life. Such advice was inflammatory and could be interpreted as traitorous. But actually it was deeply grounded in Jeremiah's consciousness that first things came first. A decade before this the "good figs" had been taken to Babylon (ch. 24). The "bad figs," so bad they could not be eaten, were the people who had been left behind in Jerusalem. What made them bad figs was their persistent rejection of the divine word. Zedekiah had despised his oath and had broken his covenant with Nebuchadnezzar (see Ezek. 17:11-21). This was declared to be equivalent to breaking his covenant with God. God had spread his net over Zedekiah, and the unhappy king would be taken in God's snare. Jeremiah had no choice: he would not be a traitor to the Lord, and so he advised the people to desert to the Chaldeans.

Jeremiah's advice was reported to the Temple officials. The prophet was promptly denounced as being worthy of death. The weak king was like clay in the hands of the princes of Judah, who preferred not to kill Jeremiah outright but sought a more indirect way of disposing of him by placing him in a cistern. Jeremiah was lowered by ropes into the cistern pit. Although it contained no water, Jeremiah immediately sank in the mire. Here he might well have perished had not the quick action of Ebed-melech, the king's Ethiopian servant, saved him. The Hebrew text of verse 9 reads, "He is dead," meaning that Jeremiah would be as good as dead if he remained there. The reference to bread probably means that Jeremiah, already weakened by his exposure, would die of hunger, for only a scanty supply of bread was now left in the city. This plea on the part of the king's servant won a favorable response from the king, who gave Ebed-melech permission to remove the prophet from the cistern. He was provided with a detail of thirty men. (The Revised Standard Version, on the authority of one Hebrew manuscript, translates the text "three.") With great care the prophet was safely lifted out of the mire and removed from the cistern.

Jeremiah's Final Interview with Zedekiah (38:14-28)

The final interview of Jeremiah with Zedekiah was both pathetic and tragic. The desperate king was ready to clutch at any straw, yet he tragically resisted the only course open to him for his own good and that of the people. At the same time Jeremiah could only confirm what he had told the king earlier in the siege (compare 21:1-7; 37:17). Secretly the king hoped Jeremiah had some favorable communication for him. He pleaded: "Hide nothing from me" (38:14). He assured Jeremiah upon oath that he would protect him from the princes (vs. 16). Once again Jeremiah urged the king to surrender himself and the city to the

Chaldeans, declaring that it was God's will to save the king and
the people from needless suffering and the city from fire. But the
king seemed to fear the Jews who had deserted to the Chaldeans.
Jeremiah urged a straightforward course, promising the king all
the protection he so earnestly desired. He also reported a vision
he had been shown by the Lord, in which the women of the
king's household were taunting the king (38:22). Did Jeremiah
still have upon him the filth of the miry pit? In any case the
women's taunts recall his remarkable deliverance from death in
the cistern. Jeremiah had been cast into the mire, but he had been
saved by a friend. Zedekiah's counselors had urged him to resist
Babylon. Having followed their advice Zedekiah was now "sunk
in the mire," but his supposed friends were leaving him to his
fate. This fate Jeremiah proceeded to describe. The royal family,
including his wives and children and the king himself, would
be seized as captives and the city would be burned with fire.

Zedekiah's weakness and fear of the princes is indicated by
his cautious exaction of secrecy from Jeremiah, a precaution
well taken, for the princes probed the prophet without delay:
"Tell us what you said to the king." The situation was a delicate
one for both king and prophet, and the answer of Jeremiah was
evasive. Was he attempting to protect himself or the king? How
much of the truth was he obliged to reveal? It is difficult to say.
His answer, however, did silence the princes. Because Jeremiah
did not tell the whole truth he concealed the real purpose of this
interview from the king's unworthy counselors. Jeremiah was thus
spared further persecution by the princes, and was allowed to
remain in the court of the guard until the day that Jerusalem
was taken by the Chaldean army.

The Fall of Jerusalem (39:1—40:6)

Jerusalem Taken by the Chaldeans (39:1-10)

The account of the fall of Jerusalem in chapter 39 parallels a
similar narrative in chapter 52 (compare II Kings 25). Here the
date is recorded when the officers of the king of Babylon entered the city. Here it is also told how Zedekiah escaped and was
captured; how he was tried and punished; how and why Jeremiah was released from the court of the guard; how Ebed-
melech was rewarded for putting his trust in the Lord; and how
Jeremiah joined Gedaliah at Mizpah.

In agreement with 52:4-7a, verses 1 and 2 indicate that the siege of Jerusalem lasted almost eighteen months. The Revised Standard Version has improved upon the translation given in other English versions by transposing correctly the last clause of chapter 38 to the opening clause of 39:3. In this way one serious ambiguity in the sense of the passage is removed. Other difficulties, however, remain to be explained. The "middle gate" (vs. 3) cannot be precisely located. It means literally, "the gate of the midst." It probably was a gate in the wall which divided Zion (the upper city) from Moriah (the lower city). Zedekiah and the soldiers who accompanied him fled from "the gate between the two walls" located at the southern extremity of the city (vs. 4). This "gate between the two walls," at the entrance of the Tyropoeon Valley, was adjacent to the Fountain Gate. It would provide access for Zedekiah into the Kidron Valley eastward toward the Jordan.

The Revised Standard Version also clarifies the reading of verse 3 by indicating that Rabsaris and Rabmag are not personal names but the titles of officers. The Rabsaris was probably the chief eunuch (officer). The title, Rabmag, has been explained incorrectly as meaning "chief of the soothsayers." It may mean "great prince." No satisfactory way has been found to reconcile the names mentioned in verse 3 with those given in verse 13. Riblah, where Zedekiah was tried after his futile escape from Jerusalem, is on the highway to Babylon above Damascus near the Lebanon range. Jeremiah had already predicted the king's unhappy fate (34:3). Sentence was pronounced upon him; his sons were slain before his eyes, as were also the nobles of Judah. Zedekiah then was blinded and bound in fetters to be taken to Babylon. Meanwhile the army of the Chaldeans burned the royal palace and the houses of the people. They also broke down the walls of the city. The survivors of the siege were deported along with those who had deserted. Only the poorest of the people were left to care for the vineyards and to till the land.

Jeremiah Is Released from the Court of the Guard (39:11-14)

The fall of the Holy City brought Jeremiah release from his confinement in the court of the guard. It appears that he was well known even to Nebuchadnezzar, who gave orders that he should be treated with consideration. Accordingly he was removed from the court of the guard and entrusted to the care of

Gedaliah. As a member of a leading family of Judah, Gedaliah
was appointed to be governor of the people who were allowed
to remain in the land. Ahikam, the father of Gedaliah, had protected Jeremiah after he had been tried for preaching the Temple Sermon (26:24). Upon the advice of Jeremiah this powerful
family had probably gone over to the Chaldeans early in the
siege. Gedaliah, in turn, had probably interceded for Jeremiah by
reporting to Nebuchadnezzar how Jeremiah had conducted himself during the siege. In any case, the prophetic activity of Jeremiah could hardly have been unknown to the Chaldeans. The city
had fallen indeed, but the prophet of Anathoth dwelt among the
people.

The Promise to Ebed-melech (39:15-18)

This item about Ebed-melech is clearly out of chronological
order since it is dated during Jeremiah's confinement in the
court of the guard. It would have followed naturally after 38:13,
where Jeremiah is said to have remained in the court of the
guard when Ebed-melech had saved him from the miry pit.
However, the main topic in the narrative of chapters 37 and 38
is concerned with the relations between Jeremiah and Zedekiah.
This personal touch between the prophet and the Ethiopian
eunuch is not inappropriate to the topical sequence of chapter
39. For, amid all the tragic consequences which followed upon
Zedekiah's infidelity, this promise to Ebed-melech shines like a
bright candle in the darkness as an illustration of fidelity. To say
that the eunuch's life would be to him as "a prize of war" means
that Ebed-melech's life would be saved, but at great peril. By
drawing Jeremiah from the miry cistern, Ebed-melech had run a
great risk of becoming a prey to Jeremiah's enemies. But Jeremiah now told him that because he had put his trust in the Lord
he was safe. The example of this Ethiopian as one who trusted
in God, and so was secure from all enemies, stands in striking
contrast to that of Zedekiah who refused to trust in the Lord and
so became a prey to his enemies the Chaldeans.

Jeremiah Chooses to Dwell at Mizpah (40:1-6)

This report of Jeremiah's release differs in certain details
from that given in 39:11-14, but in both cases it is said that
Jeremiah was committed to the care of Gedaliah and that he
dwelt among the people. According to 39:14, Nebuzaradan, the

Chaldean captain of the guard, *sent* and took Jeremiah from the court of the guard, probably by giving an order to this effect to a subordinate officer. Yet he did not actually see Jeremiah personally until the prophet was brought in chains with other captives to Ramah, some five miles north of Jerusalem, where Nebuzaradan apparently had located his headquarters. The encounter of the two men, the one a Chaldean officer of high rank, the other the captive prophet who had played a leading role during the siege of Jerusalem, is exceedingly interesting. Nebuzaradan spoke to Jeremiah as though he, too, knew the God whose will Jeremiah had proclaimed with such fidelity during his career. Was he using language he may have heard attributed to Jeremiah? At least his words agree with those Jeremiah had used to proclaim the word of the Lord (vs. 3). Nebuzaradan gave Jeremiah unrestricted liberty. Jeremiah chose to stay with the remnant of his people in their homeland. He accepted a gift of food and "a present." He then joined Gedaliah at Mizpah, where the government of the remnant had been set up.

HISTORICAL NARRATIVES (Biographic)
Jeremiah 40:7—44:30
Main Topic: Judah After the Fall of Jerusalem

Gedaliah's Murder and Its Result (40:7—43:7)

Gedaliah Governs at Mizpah (40:7-12)

The prestige of Gedaliah as governor of the remnant left in Judah is indicated by the manner in which the captains of the scattered Hebrew forces assembled about him and affirmed their loyalty to him as their chief. These men came from near and far. Two of the names in 40:8 are identified as of particular interest. Ephai came from Netophah, located in the land of Judah near Bethlehem (compare Neh. 7:26). Jezaniah came from Maacah in the land of Naphtali, southeast of Mount Hermon. In 1932 a find of outstanding interest was made at Tell en-Nashbeh. It is the seal of one "Jaazaniah, servant of the king." Can this be the very officer associated with Gedaliah? (II Kings 25:23).

Gedaliah promised to represent all the officers and people faithfully before the Chaldeans. In his first order he commanded them to gather wine and fruit and oil for storage in vessels, and to occupy their own cities. Following their example other Jews, who had taken refuge in Moab and Ammon and Edom while the Chaldeans were besieging Jerusalem, also returned to Judah and placed themselves under Gedaliah's protection.

Johanan Warns Gedaliah (40:13-16)

Among the names mentioned in 40:8 two others beside Ephai and Jezaniah are of special interest. They are Ishmael and Johanan. Ishmael, the son of Nethaniah, belonged to the house of David (41:1). He probably resented the appointment of Gedaliah, who was not a member of the royal family. At least Ishmael was in league with Baalis the king of Ammon in a plot to overthrow the pro-Chaldean government at Mizpah by taking the life of Gedaliah. Johanan, the son of Kareah, learning of this atrocious plot and fearing the consequences if it were carried out, approached Gedaliah and warned him. Also he offered to slay Ishmael secretly. Johanan knew what reprisals surely would follow if such a plot succeeded. Gedaliah, however, refused to believe this report about Ishmael. He forbade Johanan to carry out his design. Was Gedaliah too trustful, or too easygoing? His failure to take proper precautions was fatal, as succeeding events proved.

Ishmael Slays Gedaliah and Others (41:1-18)

Gedaliah not only refused to believe that Ishmael was plotting in secret against him, but even invited him to be his guest at table. While enjoying this hospitality, Ishmael and ten other conspirators "rose up and struck down Gedaliah" and all the members of the governor's retinue, including a number of Chaldean soldiers who probably were present as Gedaliah's bodyguard. If this event took place in the same year as the fall of Jerusalem it was now only three months after that tragedy. Ishmael's act was not only a violation of the Eastern law of hospitality, but was both reckless and malicious, a brutal example of the degrading effects of the prolonged siege and war against Jerusalem.

One crime tends to beget another. On the day following the murder of Gedaliah, eighty pilgrims from Shechem and Shiloh and Samaria in deep mourning approached Mizpah. They were on their way to offer sacrifices at the ruined Temple site in Jerusalem and need not have entered into Mizpah at all had they not been enticed into doing so by a ruse on the part of Ishmael, which led to their slaughter. Why he should have added this needless crime to his murder of Gedaliah is left unexplained. Ten men, however, were spared because they claimed to have hidden stores of wheat, barley, oil, and honey which might now be used by Ishmael. The bodies of the seventy slain pilgrims were cast into the large cistern at Mizpah which had been hewn by King Asa for the defense of the city. If Ishmael had intended to use this rash act as an object lesson to establish his authority as a man of action to be feared, he made a mistake, for this crime led to his undoing. As soon as the deed became known, Johanan the son of Kareah summoned other captains of the forces and together they proceeded against Mizpah. Meanwhile Ishmael had taken as his captives all the people left at Mizpah, and had set out to cross over the wilderness of Judah and the valley of the Jordan to the land of Ammon.

Johanan and his fellow captains overtook the fleeing Ishmael and his captives at Gibeon, about three miles southwest of Mizpah. Here the captives of the fleeing Ishmael abandoned him, while he and eight of his fellow conspirators made good their escape. Moved by fear of retaliation by the Chaldeans when the report of Ishmael's rash act should reach Babylon, Johanan led the unhappy remnant of people to a place near Bethlehem known as Geruth Chimham. The precise meaning of this name is obscure. Geruth may mean "inn" or "lodging place," or it may mean "sheepfolds." The name Chimham is mentioned in II Samuel 19:37-38, 40 as the name of a friend of David. It may be assumed, then, that Johanan and the remnant of Judah stopped at this lodging place near Bethlehem before determining whether or not to flee for refuge into Egypt.

The Remnant Seeks Refuge in Egypt (42:1—43:7)

Before taking such a decisive step as migrating en masse to Egypt, the leaders and the people of Judah's remnant urged Jeremiah to seek God's guidance for them. Jeremiah consented to act for them after they had given him their pledge to abide by the answer he received. Jeremiah's role as the spiritual counselor of his people had not at all been diminished by the tragic events of the preceding months.

That Jeremiah spoke only when he knew he had an authentic word from God is indicated by the fact that he waited ten days

before he was sure of the divine answer. When the answer came
he delivered it without hesitation, "The LORD has said to you, O
remnant of Judah, 'Do not go to Egypt' " (42:19). The meaning
of the words, "I repent of the evil which I did to you," is difficult for us in the Western world to grasp (42:10). But it was
not difficult for the ancient Hebrew, as the comment on 18:8
indicates. Jeremiah's address to the remnant indicates how well he
discerned the mood of his people. He anticipated the reply they
were about to make, since they apparently had determined to seek
refuge in Egypt. He assured them that they need not fear the
Chaldeans, for their God had promised to be with them to protect them. On the other hand, if they were to go to Egypt they
would do so at their own peril, for the sword, famine, and pestilence would overtake them there. Furthermore, Jeremiah counseled Judah's leaders to recognize that they had sought God's
will and that the divine answer was being faithfully given to
them. To reject the divine will when it had been declared to them
was to sin against themselves (42:20-21). Thus they would be
doubly guilty.

Jeremiah had anticipated correctly the true temper of these
leaders, for they insolently accused Jeremiah of lying to them.
They also accused Baruch, Jeremiah's faithful friend and scribe,
of conniving to deliver them into the hand of the Chaldeans by
urging them to remain in the land of Judah. The mention of the
name of Baruch at this point in the narrative is significant. It indicates that Baruch was recognized among the survivors of the
siege and fall of Jerusalem as a man of influence. Furthermore,
it shows that the link between Jeremiah and his scribe had not
been severed. If Baruch is responsible for having included in his
memoirs these events following the fall of Jerusalem, then we
have here the firsthand report of an eyewitness of the events
described.

The officers who had rallied to the support of Johanan, the
son of Kareah, all concurred in the determination to go to
Egypt. Accordingly they gathered all the people and their goods
and led them into the land of Egypt, to Tahpanhes, a royal city
on the east bank of the Pelusiac branch of the Nile River.

Jeremiah Predicts Nebuchadnezzar's Conquest of Egypt (43:8-13)

Jeremiah's prophetic gift did not leave him when he was forced to accompany the faithless remnant into Egypt. This remnant of Judah displayed the same headstrong resistance to the will of God which had brought about the fall of Jerusalem. Their determination to flee to Egypt where they would "not see war, or hear the sound of the trumpet, or be hungry for bread" (42:14), was based on a mistaken reading of the signs of their times. Shortly before this, a new Pharaoh, named Hophra, had risen to the throne of Egypt. The leaders of the remnant of Judah put their hopes in him. Under his protection they felt they would escape any reprisals from the Chaldeans for the atrocious murder of Gedaliah. By a symbolic object lesson Jeremiah now proceeded to show them how mistaken they were. In the presence of the men of Judah he took some large stones in his hands and buried them in mortar in the pavement before the entrance to the royal residence in Tahpanhes. At the same time he explained to the leaders of the remnant the meaning of this symbolic act. Nebuchadnezzar the king of Babylon was still to be regarded as God's "servant." The same instrument in the hand of God who had humbled Jerusalem would also come by divine decree to humble Egypt. In due time the king of Babylon would come and set his throne above the very stones Jeremiah had buried in the pavement. Where then would these shortsighted leaders and the pitiful remnant find security? One by one the cities of Egypt would be plucked away by the ruthless conqueror. Even the obelisks of the temple of the sun-god at Heliopolis would be destroyed. Tahpanhes, situated on the caravan route into Egypt from the north, would be one of the first cities to be taken. Indeed, within two decades after Jeremiah spoke these words the Chaldean armies appeared in Egypt on a punitive mission. Although they did not actually conquer the whole land they did overrun it.

Jeremiah's Final Message to the Jews in Egypt (44:1-30)

Now Jeremiah delivered what appears to be his last recorded prophetic message. At a gathering of Jews (probably at some

stated festival the date of which is not indicated), Jeremiah
surveyed the desolation of Jerusalem and the cities of Judah.
This overwhelming tragedy had been brought about, he declared,
because the Covenant people had persisted in the worship of
other gods. What makes this address even more significant than
its primary theme is the nature of the audience, for here representatives of all the Jews scattered throughout Egypt are said to
have been present. The expressions "land of Egypt" and "land
of Pathros" in verse 1 are doubtless meant to refer to the two
parts of Egypt, northern or Lower Egypt and southern or Upper
Egypt. Long before the fall of Jerusalem, Jews had been migrating to Egypt. Now that some pitiful survivors of the fall of
Jerusalem had arrived at Tahpanhes, these Jews would be eager
to learn from them about the recent events in their homeland.
To this mixed audience, survivors of the fall of Jerusalem and
representative Jews from Lower and Upper Egypt, Jeremiah
delivered his solemn message from the Lord.

The man from Anathoth reminded them now, as he had so
often done before the fall of the Holy City, that, despite repeated
warnings of God's servants the prophets, Judah had persisted in
worshiping false gods, and had refused to turn from this wickedness to the Covenant God. This was why their homeland and the
Holy City were now desolate. He called upon them to desist from
this practice lest a consequence still more serious come upon
them here. The sword, famine, and pestilence would consume
them in Egypt—all but a few fugitives who might some day return to the land of Judah (44:11-14). This is the essence of
Jeremiah's address (44:1-14).

But the prophet's audience was in no mood to receive these
words, for they read the recent history of Judah in an entirely
different light. According to their view, Judah had prospered
just as long as incense had been offered to the queen of heaven.
Thus they were harking back to the days of Manasseh when
Judah had been seduced into worshiping the queen of heaven
(II Kings 21:1-3). All their troubles, so it seemed to them, had
begun when Josiah made his sweeping reforms and destroyed
the cult objects of their worship (II Kings 23:4-14).

According to these men and women, the queen of heaven had
made them to prosper, as indicated in verses 17 and 18. And
outwardly, at least, so it seemed! What a catalogue of tragic
events had followed one another since Josiah's reforms! The

women insisted that their husbands were correct in attributing their prosperity to the queen of heaven, and their calamities to her wrath when they ceased to offer incense to her (vs. 19).

To Jeremiah the exact opposite was the real truth. Their obdurate practice of burning incense, Jeremiah insisted, was an affront to their God, whose long-suffering patience they had exhausted (44:22). Their desolate land was a witness against them that they had not obeyed his law. But, since this miserable remnant were determined to make profane vows and to offer pagan incense, the prophet ironically urged them to proceed upon their fatal course: "Confirm your vows and perform your vows!" (44:25). In this final picture of Jeremiah at the end of his long career we see him as a "man of sorrows, and acquainted with grief." True to his people to the end, he had chosen to remain with the remnant of Judah, even though it meant being taken with them in their flight to Egypt. Here, as he knew, only worse troubles awaited them. But, sadder yet, they too had made a choice. Their choice meant that they had rejected God's claims upon them, and consequently their privileges as the Covenant people. Only one thing remained for the prophet to say. He saw clearly that true worship of the Covenant God would cease among the Jews of Egypt (44:26). God would continue to watch over them, but now he would watch over them "for evil and not for good" (44:27). Two irreconcilable interpretations of Judah's recent history could not exist side by side. The outcome of their final choice would prove whose word would stand, Jeremiah's or theirs.

DATED DIALOGUE (Biographic)
Jeremiah 45:1-5
Main Topic: Jeremiah Counsels Baruch

Like chapter 36, this passage is dated in the fourth year of Jehoiakim. The precise language of verse 1 concerning the writing of a scroll at the dictation of Jeremiah in the same year suggests that the experience here recorded may well have accompanied the writing of the scroll described in chapter 36 (compare 36:1-2, 17-18). Chapter 45 may profitably be read, therefore, in connection with 36:8. Had the record of this incident been placed at this point in the narrative of chapter 36, however, it would have broken the carefully arranged sequence of the passage as it stands.

Whether Baruch's words, "Woe is me! for the LORD has added sorrow to my pain," indicate that he is troubled over his own immediate prospects because of his participation in the writing of the scroll, or because of the doom about to break over his people, is not clear (compare 25:27-32). But the counsel which is given to the groaning scribe has a twofold significance. First, if sorrow has been added to Baruch's pain, he is asked: What must be the Lord's sorrow over the Covenant people? For he is about to break down what he has built, he is about to uproot what he has planted (see 1:10). Let Baruch, therefore, temper his own mood in view of what the Lord painfully is obliged to do to the whole land.

Second, under these circumstances Baruch was urged to give up any personal aims to satisfy his own desires. "And do you seek great things for yourself? Seek them not" (45:5). These words certainly were not meant to stifle Baruch's initiative, or to thwart his aspirations. He would need all the initiative he could summon to survive at all in the days to come. But this counsel was rather directed to the outcome of the days just ahead. In view of what was coming, Baruch was reminded that he should be glad to get off by saving his life! The counsel to Baruch is concluded by giving him a realistic promise, "But I will give you your life as a prize of war." The expression "prize of war," used here, occurs at three other places in the Book of Jeremiah (21:9; 38:2; 39:18). The word itself refers to something which is snatched up amid danger and hurriedly borne away as a secure possession. Each time it is used in this book it refers to the life of the person involved. And so Baruch is assured that God will deliver him from the doom about to break over the Covenant people.

PROPHETIC DISCOURSES (Biographic)
Jeremiah 46:1—51:64
Main Topic: The Word of the Lord to the Nations

Introduction (46:1)

The content of chapters 46-51 consists of messages addressed to the nations. The sentence, "The word of the LORD which came

to Jeremiah the prophet concerning the nations," clearly serves
as a title to the whole collection (46:1). But as an affirmation it
has significant overtones, for it reiterates the most frequently
repeated formula in the book. Wherever this formula appears
it claims that the message it introduces is the word of the Lord,
whether it reads, "The word of the LORD came to me," or "Thus
said the LORD to me," or "Thus says the LORD." Therefore
the heading of these messages addressed to the nations makes
the same claim to divine authority heard elsewhere throughout
the whole book. But there is this difference: here the formula is
expressed in the third person, "The word of the LORD . . . to
Jeremiah the prophet," and a similar expression is used at 46:13;
47:1; and 49:34. All of which is to say that the messages addressed to Egypt (ch. 46), to Philistia (ch. 47), and to Elam
(49:34) are specifically identified as the word of the Lord spoken
to Jeremiah. Furthermore, each of these three messages has a
relation to some specific historical situation paralleling the career
of Jeremiah; as, for instance, chapter 46 to the battle of Carchemish (605 B.C.), chapter 47 to the capture of Gaza by Pharaoh Neco (after the battle of Megiddo, 609 B.C.), and 49:34-39
to the beginning of the reign of Zedekiah.

Elsewhere in these messages to the nations, however, no claim
is made for Jeremiah as the recipient of the word of the Lord.
The message is introduced, for example, with a simple statement, "Concerning Edom" (49:7); "Concerning Damascus"
(49:23); "Concerning Kedar" (49:28). Furthermore, no attempt is made in these other messages to relate them to specific situations within the lifetime of Jeremiah. It would therefore appear reasonable to assume that during the period in which
our present Book of Jeremiah was taking shape, other authentic
messages to the nations which had been preserved, besides those
delivered by Jeremiah himself, were gathered into a single collection. This collection was then permanently joined to the body
of materials already assembled from the ministry of Jeremiah.
If this took place after the Greek translation (the Septuagint)
had been made, it would account for the striking difference between the position of these messages in the Hebrew text (at the
end of the book), and their position in the Greek text (after
25:13a).

Concerning Egypt (46:2-26)

Egypt Meets God at Carchemish (46:2-12)

At Carchemish on the Euphrates in 605 B.C. the forces of Egypt were defeated by the Chaldean army. These two powers were drawn into conflict following the fall of Nineveh in 612 B.C. Pharaoh Neco led a large army of mercenaries northward from Egypt, and in 609 B.C. at Megiddo he slew Josiah king of Judah. Three years later Pharaoh Neco and Nebuchadnezzar faced each other at Carchemish. British excavations, directed by Sir C. Leonard Woolley in 1920, reveal that the fighting there was fierce. Within the ruins of a large private house hundreds of Babylonian arrowheads were found mixed with Egyptian lance points and broken swords and with other Babylonian and Egyptian relics of this period. This proves that troops of Nebuchadnezzar and Pharaoh Neco had clashed at this very spot.

The poem begins by extolling the might of Egypt and concludes with a cry over its defeat. It describes the animated preparations for battle. The Egyptian horsemen arrayed in their helmets and coats of mail are seen preparing their bucklers and shields and polishing their spears. But terror seizes them on every side (compare the similar language, 6:25; 20:3, 10; 49:29) as they flee in haste from the enemy. And so the warriors of Egypt are described as stumbling and falling by the River Euphrates.

Egypt's failure at Carchemish is made all the more striking by reason of Pharaoh Neco's proud boasts. The surging waters of the Nile each year flood the surrounding countryside. So Egypt, in the plans of Pharaoh Neco, was to rise up and cover the earth! The Egyptian king is pictured urging his mercenaries from Ethiopia and North Africa to advance into battle. But this command proved to be futile, for this was not to be Egypt's day. It was God's day! The Lord of Hosts was holding a sacrifice in the north country and the virgin daughter of Egypt was the victim. The wound Egypt received here is said to be incurable, so that no balm of Gilead, no famed medicine, could bring healing. Pharaoh Neco's claim for sovereignty in the east was denied by the Lord God of Hosts.

Nebuchadnezzar Smites Egypt (46:13-26)

The consequences of the defeat at Carchemish are now depicted. Migdol at the border, and Tahpanhes, and Memphis (the capital of Lower, that is, northern Egypt) are warned of the coming invasion. The margin of the Revised Standard Version indicates that the language of the Hebrew text here (vss. 15-16) is obscure. This translation follows the Greek Version (Septuagint) in which a contrast is drawn between the strength of Apis (the sacred bull who was supposed to be the incarnation of Osiris) and the Lord of Hosts. Because the Lord struck down Pharaoh at Carchemish, Egypt's day of opportunity to build an eastern empire had passed. In fact, Pharaoh's name was now to be called "Noisy one who lets the hour go by" (46:17). Neco had boasted that he would be like a Nile wave which covers the earth. Actually he had been like the noisy crest of a wave which breaks upon the shore only to return to the deeps from which it arose. Mount Tabor and Mount Carmel each rise above the surrounding heights. Thus, Egypt was told, the conqueror from the north would loom above all others. In view of this coming invasion the inhabitants of Memphis were urged to prepare their goods for exile (vss. 18-19).

The futility of Egypt's attempt to build an empire is made ludicrous by the metaphor of the well-nourished heifer grazing in the field but put to flight by a tiny gadfly (vs. 20). The mercenaries who had been hired to fight Egypt's battle are pictured as pampered calves who turned and fled together before the foe. The fleeing hosts of Egypt are like a hissing serpent which glides away before hewers of wood. In turn the hostile woodsmen from the north are said to be as numerous as locusts, pressing their cause and clearing away the cities of Egypt just as they would cut down a dense forest. Upper Egypt (including its famed capital at Thebes), with her gods and kings, was to be delivered into the hands of Nebuchadadnezzar and his armies. Thus the rule of the eastern world was determined at the battle of Carchemish. For Egypt it was a time of humiliation and defeat. The Lord of Hosts was proclaimed as the supreme arbiter among the nations. Nebuchadnezzar emerged as the human overlord of the whole Fertile Crescent.

Jacob to Be Saved from Afar (46:27-28)

The poem which concludes chapter 46 is a repetition of 30:10-11, in which the Covenant people are urged not to be dismayed about their captivity. He who has chastened them is described as one who in due time will prove his faithfulness by delivering them from all the nations into which he has driven them.

Concerning the Philistines (47:1-7)

Other messages directed against the Philistines are attributed to Amos (1:6-8), Isaiah (14:29-31), Ezekiel (25:15-17), Zephaniah (2:4-7), and Zechariah (9:5-7). This utterance is quite independent of the others, both in its imagery and in its emphasis. The date of the fall of Gaza and other Philistine cities cannot be precisely determined since the Pharaoh mentioned in the heading (vs. 1) may be Neco before the battle of Megiddo (609 B.C.) or after Carchemish (605 B.C.). On the other hand he may be Hophra, who made a successful northern expedition as far as Sidon.

The imagery of the poem is brilliant. The coming invasion is described as a flash flood from the north, suddenly overrunning the whole land and sweeping everything before it. Mingled with the futile crying and wailing of the inhabitants is the noise of the invader—the stamping of the war steeds, the rushing of chariots, and the rumbling of their wheels. So fierce is the onslaught that fathers forsake their children and only a few survivors escape. Why Tyre and Sidon (Phoenician cities) are mentioned is not explained, unless it is to be inferred that they were allies of the Philistine coastal cities at this time. Caphtor (vs. 4) is mentioned by Amos (9:7) as the original home of the Philistines, and probably is Crete (Ezek. 25:15-16). The inhabitants of Gaza are pictured as shaving their heads and the people of other Philistine cities as cutting themselves in grief. No cry for mercy by those who are punished can quiet the sword which the Lord has commanded to be drawn against Ashkelon and other coastal cities. The question of the people (vs. 6) is answered by the prophet (vs. 7): How can the sword be quiet when the Lord has given it a charge?

The sword here as elsewhere is the symbol of God's righteous judgment. The same judgment which fell upon Judah is directed against Judah's nearest neighbor and malignant foe. The wine cup of God's wrath which had been pressed to the lips of Jerusalem and the cities of Judah is now passed to the Philistines. They also must drink (compare 25:17-20).

Concerning Moab (48:1-47)

The length of this passage is due to the fact that it is a collection of prophetic utterances concerning Moab delivered by various prophets at different times. Verses 29-39 are parallel to corresponding parts of Isaiah 15-16, while verses 43-44 are parallel to Isaiah 24:17-18, and verses 45-46 are parallel to Numbers 21:28-29. As a prophet "concerning the nations" Jeremiah may well have reaffirmed these earlier utterances while adding to them others of his own, for the Moabites were in league with the Chaldeans during the reign of Jehoiakim (II Kings 24:2). Later, in the reign of Zedekiah, they joined with other nations in seeking to throw off the Babylonian yoke (Jer. 27). In the present form it is not possible to determine how much of this passage was actually uttered by Jeremiah and how much of it represents utterances which were gathered about Jeremiah's prophecies before the whole book as we now have it was assembled.

Not all the cities mentioned here have been identified, but the following appear on the Moabite Stone found at Dibon in 1868, on which Mesha, the King of Moab, had recorded his victories: Nebo, Horonaim, Kiriathaim, Dibon, Aroer, Jahzah, Beth-diblathaim, Beth-meon, Bozrah, and Kerioth.

The content of these utterances may be summarized as follows: The land of Moab is suffering invasion from an unnamed foe. One city after another is falling, fortresses are being broken down, and the inhabitants are in flight. Chemosh, the god of the Moabites, with his priests is helpless before the invader. Whoever fails to do the work of destruction is under the curse of God (vss. 1-10).

Moab is pictured as an easygoing land. To be settled on one's "lees" is to be content with one's lot after being long undisturbed. (To preserve its "taste" and "scent," wine was allowed to rest upon its "lees," that is, its sediment. Compare Isaiah 25:6.) Settled upon his own ways, Moab is said to have learned nothing from experience, being undisciplined and unaccustomed to hardship. Now Moab is about to be treated roughly by "tilters who will tilt him," as wine vessels are tilted for emptying, and he will be broken into pieces. Chemosh will fail Moab as Bethel and its false worship had failed Israel (see Amos 5:5; 7:10-17). Moab's best warriors and choicest young men will be slain, and the people will bewail them. The inhabitants of Dibon are cast down.

The people of Aroer seek tidings from those who escape from the foe. Moab's scepter is broken; his tableland is laid waste; his "horn," the symbol of power, is cut off and his "arm," a symbol of authority, is broken. Because Moab vaunted himself against the Lord he is to be held in derision. His arrogance will be humbled, and his boasting requited (vss. 11-27).

The inhabitants of Moab are urged to flee from the cities and to seek refuge in the rocks and gorges, because the pride, haughtiness, and insolence of Moab are under judgment. Moab's summer fruits and vineyards are despoiled. Woe is heard throughout the land; gladness and joy have ceased. Sacrifices and incense are no longer offered. Lamentations are heard on the housetops. Moab has become an object of derision and horror to all beholders (vss. 28-39).

The enemy is pictured as an eagle spreading his wings over Moab. Few escape destruction, for fear and the pit and the snare all do their destructive work. Heshbon on the north border of Moab can offer no help to the fugitives, for fire will burst forth upon them as in the days of Sihon the Amorite (Num. 21:28). In the end, however, restoration of the fortunes of Moab is promised (vss. 40-47).

Concerning Ammon (49:1-6)

The Ammonites, kinsmen of the Israelites, occupied the region east of the Jordan which surrounded Rabbah, the modern city of Amman, capital of Jordan. Under Joshua, the tribe of Gad had occupied the region known as Gilead, just to the north of the Ammonites. The deportation of the Gadites from Transjordan by Tiglath-pileser III in 733-732 B.C. (II Kings 15:29; I Chron. 5:26) gave the Ammonites an opportunity to occupy that region. This is probably the occasion to which the prophecy refers.

The question which introduces this utterance inquires about the occupation of Israelite territory. Has Israel no descendants of its own, that Ammon has occupied the cities of Gad? Milcom (a Hebrew word from the same root means "king") was the national god of the Ammonites. The day will come, so the prophet affirms, when Rabbah, the capital of Ammon, shall be made desolate and its villages burned. Then Israel once again shall regain what Ammon has appropriated.

Heshbon was located near the border just to the south of Ammon. The location of Ai in Transjordan is unknown. These cities and the inhabitants of Rabbah may well mourn and lament, says the prophet, for Milcom with his priests and princes shall go into exile. To trust in their well-watered valley, or even in their riches, will be vain, for the Lord will bring panic upon the children of Ammon and drive them away into captivity. Yet in the end the fortunes of Ammon will be restored.

Concerning Edom (49:7-22)

The correspondences between this prophecy against Edom and the Book of Obadiah are striking. Verses 9-10 are parallel to Obadiah 5-6, and verses 14-16 are parallel to Obadiah 1-4. This may indicate that each is quoting from an earlier prophet, and that each is adapting earlier words to his own specific purpose. In any case, there is a remarkable concurrence between these utterances and Ezekiel 25:12-14; Psalm 137:7; and Lamentations 4:21. The readiness of Edom to take advantage of the fall of Jerusalem in 587 B.C. by occupying cities in the south of Judah was deeply resented by the Israelites and doubtless inspired the malignant cry of hate in Psalm 137:7 and Obadiah 10-14.

Teman was most likely a district in north Edom, since Dedan was located south of Edom in Arabia (compare Ezek. 25:13). The questions posed in verses 7-9 call attention to a sudden and complete calamity which is about to overtake Edom. The prophet's imagery of the grape-gatherers and thieves, and his references to hiding places and fatherless children, all indicate how thorough he expects Edom's coming judgment to be. Like all the nations, Edom must drink of the cup (see 25:17-26). Bozrah, 25 miles southeast of the Dead Sea, shall be laid waste (compare 48:21-26). A messenger of the Lord has been sent to stir up the nations against Edom. Edom's lofty cliffs will provide no security, for the coming destruction will be as complete as that of Sodom and Gomorrah. Like helpless sheep fleeing from a lion, the inhabitants of Edom will be driven before the invader. The sound of Edom's fall will cause the earth to tremble. Like a victim upon whom an eagle swoops down, the warriors of Edom shall faint. Did Malachi refer to this judgment as already accomplished? His words in 1:2-5 imply it.

Concerning Damascus (49:23-27)

Damascus is not mentioned in 25:17-26 as among those nations compelled to drink the cup of God's wrath; neither is it
possible to determine why this utterance should be included here.
No specific historical occasion for the prophecy is stated, and
the name of no foe is mentioned. Verse 24b recalls 6:24; verse
26 parallels 50:30; and verse 27 is parallel to Amos 1:4.

Hamath is about one hundred miles north of Damascus, and
Arpad is about twice as far. The inhabitants of these cities
are said to be confounded over the evil tidings brought to them
of the fall of Damascus. They are troubled like the restless sea.
Damascus itself is described as enfeebled and paralyzed and in
anguish before the foe. This famed city is forsaken, for its de-
fenders have fallen. God has kindled a fire which devours the
city. Ben-hadad was the name of several kings of Syria (I Kings
15:18-20; II Kings 13:24).

Concerning Kedar and Hazor (49:28-33)

Kedar is the name of a nomadic tribe living in the Syro-
Arabian desert. It is mentioned in Isaiah 21:16; 60:7; Jeremiah
2:10; and Ezekiel 27:21. Several Hazors are located in Palestine, but here the term is doubtless used in a collective sense for
seminomadic Arabs, since they are also spoken of as "the people
of the east" (49:28). Kedar's tents and flocks, curtains and goods
and camels, all are to be borne away by the foe. Nebuchadnezzar
is summoned to smite the inhabitants of Hazor and is promised
an easy victory, with spoils of flocks, and booty of camels and
cattle. The inhabitants are warned to flee, but Hazor itself is
doomed to oblivion.

Concerning Elam (49:34-39)

This is the only utterance among those addressed to foreign
nations that is dated in the reign of Zedekiah. Elam was located
in the hill country east of Babylon. Susa was its capital. Because
of the deportation of Jehoiachin and some ten thousand captives
to Babylon in 597 B.C. (see II Kings 24:10-16), interest in the
destiny of neighboring Elam would be strong among the Jews.
Here the prophet declares that the military might ("bow")

of Elam will be broken, and its people will be scattered to the four winds. The people of Elam will be terrified before their enemies, and the sword of the Lord will consume them. God will set up his throne in Elam to judge and destroy the king and princes. Yet in the latter days Elam shall be restored. Ezekiel records the overthrow of Elam (32:24). The exiles would not derive much comfort from this utterance concerning Elam if they had set their hopes of deliverance on help from this direction.

Concerning Babylon (50:1—51:64)

Although the prophecy concerning Babylon (chs. 50-51) follows those addressed to other foreign nations (chs. 46-49), its only immediate connection with them is topical; that is to say, it is chiefly a message of judgment addressed to a foreign nation. But it is strikingly different from the other foreign nations' messages in three ways:

1. Its timing is distinctly that of the Exile. The Temple has been desecrated by aliens (50:28; 51:11, 51). The Covenant people, including both Israel and Judah, are in exile (50:4-5, 8, 20, 28, 33; 51:34, 50).

2. Its viewpoint is in contrast to Jeremiah's emphasis at the turning point of his career (25:1-13). At that time (see also chapters 46 and 47) Nebuchadnezzar had just emerged as the overlord over the whole Near Eastern world, and Babylon was proclaimed as the instrument of the Lord's judgment. Only a hint was given that Babylon would be judged (25:12-13, 26). Now, however, the fall of Babylon is proclaimed to be imminent, and the land of the Chaldeans is to be plundered (50:8-10, 45-46). The days of Nebuchadnezzar's ascendancy are a thing of the past (50:17-18; 51:34). The Medes are mentioned as the foe destined to overthrow Babylon (51:11). The deliverance of the Covenant people is near at hand (50:17-19).

3. The spirit of these prophecies concerning Babylon is passionate and vindictive. Jeremiah's emphasis at mid-career had been moderate. Nebuchadnezzar was declared to be the Lord's "servant," although in due time he would come under judgment. Now the time is said to be here; vengeance is to fall on Babylon.

Thus by timing, viewpoint, and spirit the content of chapters 50 and 51 is quite distinctive. It is appropriate, however, that the messages concerning foreign nations should be concluded topically by these prophetic utterances about Babylon, even though they cannot be identified as Jeremiah's. Although these messages represent a wide chronological gap between the prophecies of Jeremiah and their fulfillment, they do have an appropriate place here as an appendix to the whole book.

Another feature of these chapters is their disorganized arrangement of parts. The contents are presented now in poetry, now as prose. The format of the Revised Standard Version clearly indicates this. The messages represent a variety of occasions. The style suggests a number of speakers. No attempt has been made to arrange these messages in any discernible sequence, but the attention of the speakers alternates between two dominant themes, the announcement of Babylon's approaching doom and the proclamation of Israel's certain deliverance.

The passages which develop the theme of Babylon's doom are 50:2-3, 8-16, 21-46; 51:1-14, 20-58, 59-64. But alternating with this note on Babylon's doom is the proclamation of deliverance for the Covenant people. The two houses are addressed either as the "people of Israel" or the "people of Judah" in 50:4-7, 17-20, 33-34. A similar note is also sounded in 51:15-19. Although there is no progressive sequence of parts here, the alternation of emphasis on the coming fall of Babylon and the return of the Covenant people to their own land lends a touch of unity to this whole collection, which is entitled, "The word which the LORD spoke concerning Babylon."

The words "by Jeremiah the prophet" in the title (50:1) must therefore be interpreted in the light of the whole context, historical, theological, personal. In one sense these utterances can be said to be "by Jeremiah," since so many of the sentences repeat his own words (for instance, compare 50:3 with 4:6-7; 50:7 with 2:3; and 51:43 with 2:6). In another sense the utterances can only be said to be "by Jeremiah" insofar as they are the fulfillment of his prophecies brought to pass after his own days (for instance, compare 51:26 with 25:12 and 51:41 with 25:26).

Chapters 50 and 51 clearly are an exilic addition to the book, proclaiming judgment upon Babylon in fulfillment of Jeremiah's words, and also announcing a return of the Covenant people to their own land.

Babylon Judged; Israel and Judah Redeemed (50:1—51:58)

The prophecy begins by describing the dismay of the gods of Babylon over the desolation that is overtaking their city. Bel means "Lord," but the term came to be used also as a proper name. The patron deity of Babylon was Marduk ("Merodach"). The main theme of this collection having been introduced (50: 2-3), the alternating theme is also announced. A penitent Israel and Judah are described as seeking the Lord their God. They are seen as inquiring the way to Zion that they may join themselves to the Covenant God (50:4-5). Like lost sheep led astray by false shepherds, God's people had "forgotten" their fold. They were devoured by enemies who pointed to Israel's sins as the cause of her present captivity (50:6-7).

An assembly of nations from the north is summoned to destroy Babylon so completely that the land will be reduced to a wilderness. Babylon's enemies are invited to hew her down as a sign of the Lord's vengeance against her sins (50:8-16).

First Assyria devoured Israel (722-21 B.C.). Then Nebuchadnezzar crushed the kingdom of Judah (587 B.C.). Assyria was punished when Nineveh fell in 612 B.C. Now it is said to be Babylon's turn to be judged. But Israel and Judah who have suffered for their sins are about to be restored (50:17-20).

"Merathaim," meaning "visitation" or "punishment" (see 50: 27; 51:18), was an Aramean tribe which occupied the region near the mouth of the Tigris River eastward from Babylon. Both lands and their peoples are declared to be ready for destruction. Babylon, once the "hammer" of the Lord, is now to be broken and despoiled (50:21-32).

The Hebrew word translated "Redeemer" (50:34) means "near kinsman." By the use of this term for the Lord of Hosts, Israel and Judah are reminded that the Covenant God, faithful to his people, will plead their cause and provide for their deliverance from their present captivity (50:33-34).

The sword of judgment is summoned to fall upon the Chaldeans—upon the people themselves, their weapons, their treasures, and their waters. The idols and images in which Babylon boasts cannot deliver the city. The coming destruction of Babylon will be as complete and perpetual as that of Sodom and Gomorrah. The enemy from the north will despoil the city (compare 6:22-24) and the tidings of her fall will be heard by all the nations. What happened to Edom (49:19-21) will also happen to Babylon. The enemy like a lion from the jungle will despoil her (50:35-46).

The destroying enemy of Babylon is described as a winnower who fans away chaff, and as an archer whose arrows can penetrate a defender's coat of mail. Israel and Judah are assured that they are not forsaken, for the judgment of Babylon is at hand (51:1-5). Although Babylon was like "a golden cup in the Lord's hand" whose contents made the nations mad, the time of judgment has come. No balm for her healing can be found. By the decree of the Lord (51:6-14) the Medes will be the instrument of the Lord's vengeance.

At this point a passage is inserted into these utterances which is also found in Jeremiah 10:12-16. Although these words (51: 15-19) interrupt the sequence of thought, they emphasize the impotence of Babylon's idols against the Lord of Hosts. Magnifying the Lord's power, wisdom, and understanding against the worthlessness of Babylon's graven images, the words add to the effectiveness of the following poem, which seems to be addressed to the unnamed conqueror (presumably the Medes, 51: 11) who now becomes the "hammer and weapon of war" in the hand of the Lord to requite Babylon for the evil done in Zion (51:20-24).

The designation of Babylon as a destroying mountain is probably meant to suggest that Babylon had exalted herself over other nations to corrupt them (51:53). But the lot of Babylon now is said to be that of a perpetual waste. Ararat and Minni were districts in Armenia. Ashkenaz was probably an adjacent district. As the Medes approach the doomed city, couriers are sent from every quarter to relay word of their progress to the king of Babylon. Like a threshing floor, Babylon is prepared for the harvest of her ill deeds. Among these deeds Nebuchadnezzar's violence against Zion is mentioned. Jerusalem cries for vengeance, and the Lord replies that Babylon shall become a heap of ruins. Babylon will cease to exult over the spoils taken by violence. Instead the Lord will prepare a feast which will induce a swoon from which Babylon will never recover (51: 25-40).

This collection of miscellaneous utterances concerning Babylon is concluded by a further outburst. Babylon, once the praise of the whole earth for its magnificence, is now described as engulfed by the waves of the sea. Bel, the patron deity, is compelled to eject the treasures he has swallowed. Rumor at last will give way to fact and Babylon will utterly collapse, thus bringing joy to heaven and earth. The captives are urged to escape from the doomed city, but they reply that aliens have desecrated their holy places. Whereupon the Lord decrees judgment. Though Babylon should mount to heaven no device could save her, for the Lord will requite the violence of Babylon by leveling her broad walls to the ground. The prophecies end on a solemn note: "the nations weary themselves only for fire" (51:41-58).

Zedekiah's Visit to Babylon (51:59-64)

In the fourth year of his reign Zedekiah made an official visit to Babylon. No reason is given for his mission, although when this passage is compared with 27:2-11, it may be inferred that he had been summoned to the Babylonian court to account for the visit of foreign ambassadors to Zedekiah's capital, presumably to form an alliance against Babylon. Zedekiah was accompanied on this visit by Seraiah, the son of Neriah, a brother of Baruch, Jeremiah's scribe. Jeremiah asked Seraiah to take with him a scroll on which was written the doom of Babylon. After reading it aloud, Seraiah was to pray, by way of confirming what he had read. He was then to bind a stone to the scroll and cast it into the Euphrates. By this act he was to symbolize the fate which was in due time to overtake Babylon. As he cast it into the waters he was to say, "Thus shall Babylon sink, to rise no more, because of the evil that I am bringing upon her."

This symbolic act, although lifted out of its earlier historical context, is placed here as a sort of topical climax to the whole exilic collection, which itself strikingly confirms what Jeremiah in the fourth year of Zedekiah had predicted would come to pass.

HISTORICAL APPENDIX (Biographic)
Jeremiah 52:1-34
Main Topic: The Fall of Jerusalem

Jeremiah 52:1-34 and 39:1-14 present reminiscences of the fall of Jerusalem which are parallel to II Kings 24:18—25:30. It would appear that these materials have been drawn from some common source. Jeremiah 52 omits II Kings 25:22-26, concerning the appointment of Gedaliah as governor, but adds, in verses 28-30, an item concerning various deportations of Jews. The content of Jeremiah 52 emphasizes the appointment of Zedekiah, the famine during the siege, the destruction of the city and Temple, the list of officials and others slain at Riblah, and the enumeration of captives taken in certain dated deportations.

For the occasion of Zedekiah's enthronement the reader is referred to II Kings 24:17, which precedes a summary of Zedekiah's reign parallel to this opening paragraph of Jeremiah 52. A vivid picture of Zedekiah's infidelity to his oath of allegiance to Nebuchadnezzar is presented in Ezekiel 17.

The extremities to which Jerusalem was reduced in the famine during the siege are described in Lamentations 2:20-22; 4:1-20. The events mentioned in connection with the fall of Jerusalem according to verses 4-16 are summarized in the parallel account in Jeremiah 39:1-10.

The pillars of bronze and other Temple furnishings are described in detail in I Kings 7:13-51. Some Temple vessels had already been taken to Babylon (Jer. 27:16-22 and 28:1-16). The pillars were broken up (52:17), and the remainder of the furnishings were taken to Babylon. Seraiah, the chief priest, was the grandfather of Jeshua, a high priest after the Exile (I Chron. 6:14; Ezra 3:2) and an ancestor of Ezra (Ezra 7:1). Zephaniah is mentioned in Jeremiah 21:1; 29:24-32; and 37:3. The leaders here mentioned had actively resisted Babylonian rule, a policy which now proved fatal for them.

The enumeration of captives given in verses 28-30 is a distinct addition to the several accounts of the fall of Jerusalem. Apparently it is drawn from some independent source of information which refers in a fragmentary way to three different deportations. The first of these is dated in the seventh year of Nebuchadnezzar's reign (598-597 B.C.), the second in the eighteenth year (587 B.C.), and the third, five years after the fall of the city when, according to Josephus, stragglers in the country were rounded up.

The last item in chapter 52 refers to the restoration of Jehoiachin to royal favor, and thus gives a hopeful note to the closing chapter of Jeremiah. Evil-merodach, the son and successor of Nebuchadnezzar, restored Jehoiachin to limited freedom by admitting him to his own table, but kept him as a member of his court. Although this favor was shown to Jehoiachin, he was doomed to have no direct successor upon the throne of David.

THE LAMENTATIONS

OF JEREMIAH

INTRODUCTION

The overwhelming tragedy which engulfed the kingdom of Judah in 587 B.C., when Jerusalem was leveled to rubble and the Covenant people were deported or scattered, left in its wake many staggering questions. How could the Covenant God allow the Holy City to be destroyed? Was he impotent or did he no longer care about his people? Had he after all forsaken them? Had his promises failed? How could the sufferings of these exiles be alleviated? Amid their despair could they possibly find any prospect of a future deliverance? Dared they expect to be established once again in their homeland? And would justice ever be meted out to their tormentors?

Five poems composed during the Exile, entitled in our English versions The Lamentations of Jeremiah, give realistic answers to such urgent questions. These five lyric utterances represent far more than the bitter sobs of any single individual over a fallen city. The torrents of emotion which surge through these poems exhibit in verse form the collective outpourings of a people whose sufferings served to intensify their sense of a divinely appointed destiny in history. The nation they adored had been dashed to pieces, but the spirit of these people, though broken in grief and appalled by guilt, was now set free to make a new beginning.

Although the burden of the five poems is the present afflictions and bitterness of the Covenant people, there are lines which recall "all the precious things" that were theirs from days of old (1:7). Here and there plaintive cries are heard, "O LORD, behold my affliction" (1:9); "Look, O LORD, and see!" (2:20); "Remember, O LORD, what has befallen us" (5:1). Occasionally a single expression of confidence gives a glimmer of hope, "The LORD is my portion . . . therefore I will hope in him" (3:24); "But thou, O LORD, dost reign for ever . . . Renew our days as of old!" (5:19, 21). Thus, although the calamities of the present provide the dominant mood of these verses, both retrospect and prospect play a significant role in molding their emotional tone. The mood shifts from grief to guilt and even to vindictiveness. But amid these fluctuations of spirit, submission turns to confession, and a whisper of confidence in the faithfulness of the Covenant God swells to a fervent exclamation of hope in his unfailing goodness (3:22-24).

The Authorship of the Poems

Whether or not Jeremiah wrote these poems is difficult to prove. The title in the English versions ascribes their authorship to Jeremiah in accordance with a preface affixed to the Greek translation. But the internal evidence for single authorship of all five poems is far from conclusive. The reader interested in these questions should turn to the more technical commentaries for aid in evaluating this evidence. As an eyewitness of the fall of Jerusalem, Jeremiah could well have written poems two and four. Quite obviously he is the person described in poem three if he is not actually the speaker (see comment). Poems one and five represent a point of view somewhat more distant from the fall of the Holy City, yet sufficiently near to contemplate the after-effects.

The Character and Purpose of the Poems

The confessional character of all five poems is closely connected with their clearly liturgical purpose. In fact, these dual features appear to account for the way in which the elegies came to be composed at all. Each poem is an ideal interpretation of the deeper meaning of the national disaster which overtook the Jewish people in 587 B.C. They are poignant litanies of grief mingled with communal confessions of guilt and heart-rending cries for mercy. Such lyric elegies as these were powerfully designed to mold the convictions, to deepen the sense of personal responsibility, and to elevate the outlook of the Covenant people upon their immediate circumstances and coming destiny. It is not at all strange therefore that the Lamentations have exercised a potent influence upon the Jewish people down through the centuries. In the Hebrew Bible, Lamentations is reckoned among the Five Rolls: Ruth, Song of Solomon, Ecclesiastes, Lamentations,

Esther. As a single book these elegies are identified in the Hebrew Bible by the first word of the first poem: "How . . . !" (repeated in 2:1 and 4:1).

The enduring significance of the Lamentations as a unit of Holy Scripture is indicated by the use made of these poems in the synagogue service on the ninth day of the fifth month (Ab) when the destruction of the ancient Temple is commemorated. In the Roman Church, passages from Lamentations are read on the last three days of Holy Week, as they are also in certain Protestant liturgies on the same days, and in some also on the Tenth Sunday after Trinity.

The Structure of the Poems

At first sight the structure of these poems may seem somewhat artificial to the average reader, since the first two and last two consist of twenty-two verses while the third has sixty-six (three times twenty-two). Actually, in their Hebrew form these poems are alphabetic. Each successive stanza of the first four poems begins with a different letter of the Hebrew alphabet. The fifth poem does not follow this acrostic scheme, even though it has twenty-two verses. Various reasons may be given for the acrostic arrangement. Would such an order be an aid to memory? Perhaps. The rising and falling inflection which characterizes elegiac meter, while it tends to become somewhat monotonous, would at the same time be a distinct aid to the memory. Or is it possible that the acrostic arrangement was deliberately chosen to keep the surcharged emotional element of the poems under control? If so, the poems are a striking example of balance between form and spirit in lyrical composition. But it has also been suggested that the alphabetical arrangement gives a sense of continuity and completeness to the communal expressions of grief and guilt and striving for hope which these elegies encouraged. The degree to which such intentions have been actualized in these moving elegies, any present-day reader may readily discover for himself. Since these elegies appear to have been designed for use in public worship, and because they appeal directly to the susceptibilities of the hearer, no extensive attempt is made here to explain what they mean. The following observations on the content and structure of the poems will make the present-day reader more fully aware of what they were originally intended to be.

COMMENTARY

"How lonely sits the city" (1:1-22)

The first part of the poem (1:1-11), written in the third person, is descriptive. The Covenant people, whether referred to as "the city," "Judah," "the daughter of Zion," or "Jerusalem," are personified in the guise of a widow—alone, tributary, betrayed, desolate, bitter, filthy, despised. Once she was "a princess among the cities." Now she dwells alone; "she weeps bitterly in the night." All her former glory has vanished; the treasures of her heritage, "the appointed feasts," have ceased; "she has seen the nations invade her sanctuary." All this is due, she acknowledges, to "the multitude of her transgressions," because she "sinned grievously" and "took no thought of her doom."

Suddenly this descriptive setting (1:1-11) shifts to a close-up, spotlighted lament of the widow herself (1:12-22). Her voice is heard in a pathetic cry of anguish: "Is it nothing to you, all you who pass by?" (vs. 12). Two plaintive prayers which anticipate this cry have already been heard from the lips of the widow in verses 9 and 11. Now the full torrent of her overwhelming grief flows unchecked. Yet in all this outpouring of grief not a single note of resentment is heard. Instead the widow frankly admits that her tragic undoing is all her own fault—she had been rebellious. At the same time she confesses: "The LORD is in the right" (vs. 18). This confession, heard in such a melancholy setting, is made all the more poignant by the confirming voice in verse 17, spoken as though by some judicious observer.

This note introduces the finale of this elegy in the form of a passionate prayer centered in the words of verse 21. The concluding lines become a plea for redress: "Deal with them as thou hast dealt with me." The widow's soul is in tumult and her heart is wrung and faint while she pleads that the taunts of her foes shall be requited. If it be true that the Lord has done it, then they too must bow before his justice.

"How the Lord in his anger . . . has done what he purposed" (2:1-22)

This elegy, like the first, is an acrostic in which each three-line stanza is begun by a different Hebrew letter. But here, as in chapters 3 and 4, the order of the sixteenth and seventeenth letters for some reason is reversed, although no shift in the thought order of the stanzas is discernible.

The first part (2:1-10) is a vivid eyewitness portrayal of the fall of Jerusalem in which the speaker depicts how palace and stronghold, altar and sanctuary, ramparts and walls, gates and bars, are broken down under the might of a relentless hand. The splendor of Zion is beclouded. The habitations of Jacob are broken down. The might of Israel is cut off. The kingdom and its rulers are dishonored. The king and princes are captured. Prophet and priest are silenced. The elders and maidens of Jerusalem are bowed to the ground. What is most singular about all this is that the Lord is pictured as the enemy! He himself has initiated and executed the action. His anger has been poured out on the daughter of Zion. "He has bent his bow like an enemy." He has determined to lay Zion in ruins. He has not restrained his hand from destroying.

The second part (2:11-22) becomes even more pointed as the sufferings of the people during the siege are described. Some starving children swoon with hunger in the streets, others find no nourishment at their mothers' breasts. Zion's ruin, beyond human aid, is seen to be as vast as the ocean in its scope. This overwhelming judgment is viewed as a direct consequence of the deceptive visions of the false prophets and their misleading oracles. Well may travelers hiss and wag their heads and cry out in amazement over the ruin of the city (2:15). This day of terror, marked by the enemy's destruction of the Holy City, is declared to be but what the Lord himself had purposed. Well may the daughter of Zion give herself no respite, but pour out her heart at every watch hour of the night for the lives of her children.

But is God really as relentless and obdurate as these acts would imply? What makes this outpouring of grief amid Zion's ruin so moving is the fact that the daughter of Zion does not blame God for her woes. Rather she recognizes the futility of seeking relief from any source except him. If he has smitten the innocent so sorely, will he not give heed to Zion's cry in the night for a reversal of her doom? "Look, O LORD, and see!" Surely God cannot be unconcerned about the slaughter of young and old in the streets. Nor can he be indifferent to those in the Holy City who are met by terrors on every side and by the implacable sword of the enemy.

"I am the man who has seen affliction" (3:1-66)

As in chapters one and two, the meter of the third poem is elegiac. But the acrostic form is somewhat different. The sixty-six lines are arranged by triplets into twenty-two stanzas, but each line of every triplet begins with the same initial letter. The main parts of the whole composition may be viewed in two different ways.

First, when viewed in terms of a speaker, there are three parts. (1) In verses 1-39 an individual "I" ("me," "my") speaks concerning "him" ("he," "his"). (2) In verses 40-47 the singular "I" changes to the plural "We" ("us," "our") and the voice of the individual is blended with that of his suffering, confessing people. (3) In verses 48-66, once again the individual "I" ("my," "me") speaks, while addressing himself to the Lord.

Second, when viewed in terms of topic the poem has four main parts. (1) A Cry of Despair (3:1-18). A sorely afflicted person, who refers to himself in the words "I am the man," voices his despair over the extremity and persistence of his sufferings under the hand of his adversary (3:1-3) and under his own people, who have made him a laughingstock (3:14). (2) A Psalm of Hope (3:19-39). Here the speaker contemplates the mercies of God. He addresses the Lord twice as "the Most High" (3:35, 38), and refers to himself as a mere "man" (3:27, 35, 39). He then concludes that good and evil come "from the mouth of the Most High" (3:38-39). (3) A Prayer of Penitence (3:40-47). Here the stricken people to whom the individual belongs describe themselves as "offscouring and refuse," and urge one another to examine their ways and return to the Lord. (4) A Prayer for Deliverance and Requital (3:48-66). Once more the individual is heard: "Judge thou my cause" (3:59). The conviction that God has seen the wrong done to him, backed by an earnest plea for justice, leads the speaker to believe that divine retribution will fall upon his enemies (3:59-66).

Thus it may be seen that this third poem differs from the first two in both form and composition. It certainly is the most profound and personal of the five elegies. Beginning with the opening affirmation, "I am the man," the imagery used to describe the personal afflictions of the speaker conveys the impression of acute suffering, unparalleled agony, and utter despair. The extremities of this identified sufferer mount in degree and pathos.

Whoever the man is, he pictures himself as tormented willfully and relentlessly by none other than God (see 3:12). Whether the speaker actually is Jeremiah, or someone who sympathetically understood his inner feelings and personal experiences, cannot be precisely determined, but the terms and phrases used remind the reader very definitely of Jeremiah (compare vs. 14 with Jer. 20:7; vs. 48 with Jer. 9:1, 18; vs. 53 with Jer. 38:6-13). The speaker has tasted bitterness and wormwood and gall! Yet he is not left entirely without hope.

Does the mood of the sufferer change at verse 20, or at verse 21? The Hebrew of verse 20 is ambiguous. It would appear that a change of mood on the part of the speaker came when he recognized himself, despite "the wormwood and the gall," as still being the object of God's incomprehensible care. The sufferer could make no claims on God, for he had sinned and rebelled against God deliberately. And God had sent relentless judgment. But this did not mean that the Covenant people were forsaken. Far from it. It meant that the Covenant God still had a claim upon his people. They had been brazenly faithless; he, however, remained steadfastly faithful. Therefore they could confess with confidence his steadfast love, his mercies, and his faithfulness (3:22-24). To confide in the initiative and fidelity of the Covenant God is the spring of Israel's hope! This is the comfort which this elegy holds out to the afflicted exiles. This ray of Covenant love from the Covenant God becomes a gleam of hope to the Covenant people. They may quietly wait for the Lord in the confidence that "he does not willingly afflict . . . the sons of men" (3:33).

Where will one find a more revealing clue to the change of fortune which overtook the stricken exiles when at the heart of their life such signs of returning health and hope began to pulse? And who can begin to estimate the influence of these remarkable elegies upon the sons of Zion, across the years, as such stanzas as these have been intoned in the synagogue service?

"How the gold has grown dim . . . !" (4:1-22)

This poem, like the first two, is an acrostic, but differs from them in that its stanzas consist of two lines instead of three. Here also the sixteenth and seventeenth letters of the Hebrew alphabet are reversed, but without any interruption in the thought sequence of the stanzas. No satisfactory explanation of this curious reversal has as yet been given.

The poem falls into four parts. (1) In verses 1-10 an eye-witness depicts the horrors of the siege which engulfed all classes of the people. (2) Verses 11-16 attribute the cause of this over-whelming calamity to the iniquities of the prophets and priests. (3) Verses 17-20 (compare Jer. 37:6-10) describe the vain hopes of the besieged citizenry for deliverance, and the futile attempt of the faithless king to escape. (4) Verses 21 and 22 rebuke the neighboring Edomites for gloating over the fall of the Holy City.

The most striking feature of this poem is the contrast drawn between the former glory of the Holy City and its present deso-lation. The city itself is like tarnished gold, and its precious stones, once devoted to a holy purpose, are scattered. As for the sons of Zion, once esteemed to be of great worth, they are now debased like earthen sherds. Mothers, deranged by suffering, have become inhuman. Their nurslings are parched, their chil-dren are unfed. Those who were accustomed to delicacies are faint with hunger, while those who were clad royally now grovel in ashes. The sufferings of the heinous sinners of Sodom were mo-mentary as compared to the prolonged chastisement now justly in-flicted upon the Covenant people. The nobles of Zion, once re-nowned for their healthy appearance, are now blacker than soot and shriveled like a stick. Under these conditions it would be better far to be slain by the sword than to be consumed by hunger. The hands of the women, accustomed to practice kindly deeds, now, under torments of famine, have boiled their own children for food. Prophets and priests who condemned just per-sons to death now are defiled with blood. Once they were hon-ored people. Now as unclean men they are compelled to flee away as though leprous. Even the king (Zedekiah), known as "the breath of our nostrils, the LORD's anointed," was pursued and trapped like an animal in a hunter's pit (compare Jer. 39: 4-7).

The note on which this poem closes re-echoes a strain heard in the previous poems. It is asserted that the daughter of Zion has been compelled to drink the cup of the Lord's wrath, and justly. But it is also claimed that the God who has smitten his people will visit them with deliverance from exile (4:22; see also 3:31-36; 5:21). Having poured out his wrath by enkindling a fire in Zion which consumed the foundations of the city and destroyed its gates (4:11-12), God will restore his people. The iniquity of the daughter of Zion has been punished, her warfare is accomplished, and she has made satisfaction for her guilt (4:22). But this same note of promise to Zion pulses as well with the certainty of retribution for the Edomites. The daughter of Edom must drink also from this cup of the Lord's wrath (4:21). Although the foundations of Zion have been shaken, the Lord's sovereignty over the world assures the outworking of his designs for the Covenant people.

"Remember, O Lord, what has befallen us" (5:1-22)

In this concluding poem the acrostic pattern is abandoned, but there are again twenty-two lines. Each line is composed of two balanced halves which correspond to each other in rhythm and thought-form. The artistic appeal in range of feeling and lyric expression is fully as impressive as in the preceding poems.

Verse 1 introduces a prayer in which the Lord is entreated to consider the disgrace which has befallen the Covenant people, who are said to be dispossessed as orphans (5:2-3), afflicted and persecuted as slaves (5:4-10). The sufferings of women and virgins, princes and elders, young men and old men, are affirmed to be appalling (5:11-14). Deep depression has settled down upon all classes; Zion lies desolate, and foxes prowl in its ruins (5:15-18). The poem concludes on a note of expectation. The Lord's throne endures forever. Surely he will not continually forget his people. Will he not renew their days as of old? He cannot be angry forever (5:19-22).

The confessional character of this concluding poem is perhaps its most striking characteristic. The indignations heaped upon the people of Judah, severe as they are, are recognized as just. Yet the desperate condition of these people is not regarded as irremediable. The afflictions described here would appear to be those suffered by the miserable remnant of the people left in the land by the Chaldean forces after the fall of Jerusalem (5:3, 17-18). The woes of this remnant are attributed by them to be the consequence of their sins (5:16). But they are confident that the Lord is sovereign over all his works and for all time:

> "But thou, O LORD, dost reign for ever;
> thy throne endures to all generations" (5:19).

We are reminded in this remarkable utterance how hope is begotten amid conditions of despair. The appalling adversities of the Covenant people did not extinguish the flame of faith, but instead replenished its resources when the stricken people reasserted their trust in the revealed character of the Covenant God whose glorious nature is declared in the Law and proclaimed by the prophets.